# PASTA
## EVERY WAY FOR EVERY DAY

# PASTA
## EVERY WAY FOR EVERY DAY
### Eric Treuillé & Anna Del Conte

PHOTOGRAPHY BY IAN O'LEARY

DK

**DK**

## Dorling Kindersley
LONDON, NEW YORK, MELBOURNE,
MUNICH and DELHI

**NEW EDITION**

DTP DESIGNER
Mar Villaneuva
PRODUCTION EDITOR
Jenny Woodcock
PRODUCTION CONTROLLER
Mandy Inness

**ORIGINAL EDITION**

EDITORIAL CONSULTANT
Rosie Kindersley
DESIGN AND ART DIRECTION
Stuart Jackman
PROJECT EDITOR
Julia Pemberton Hellums
EDITOR
Sally Somers
ASSISTANT EDITOR
Anna Brandenburger
PRODUCTION CONTROLLER
Elizabeth Cherry
FOOD STYLING
Eric Treuillé

First published in Great Britain in 2000
Reissued in Great Britain in 2008 by
Dorling Kindersley Limited,
80 Strand, London WC2R 0RL

A CIP catalogue record for this book is
available from the British Library

ISBN 978-1-4053-3209-5

Printed and bound by
Sheck Wah Tong Printing Press Ltd, China

discover more at
**www.dk.com**

# CONTENTS

# INTRODUCTION

The Italians, who are masters at combining sophistication with simplicity, have eaten pasta over the past millennium. They know that no other food can nourish and delight so easily, while asking for so small an effort on the part of the cook. Simple yet sustaining, a dish of pasta satisfies our hunger yet invites the eye and pleases the palate with its countless shapes, colours and flavours. It is the most versatile of foods, changing its character with ease, according to season, occasion, cook's mood or time available.

In this book we concentrate mainly on dried pasta, which is the pasta that the Italians eat religiously and lovingly every day of every week. It is the pasta they always have on hand, and it is the pasta that pairs most successfully with the greatest number of different sauces.

Some of the sauces we have chosen are classic, others are modern and many are variations on a traditional theme. There are slow-simmered sauces that can be prepared totally ahead of time, as well as many quick-fix sauces that can be made just before eating, so a whole meal can be put together in half an hour or less. Put together, yes, but always with love, care and attention.

When the family is ready to eat, the pasta slides into a pan full of boiling water, and the cook shouts *Ho messo giù la pasta* - I've put the pasta in. A few minutes later everyone sits down in silence and the cook brings in the bowl of steaming pasta and sets it in the middle of the table for people to serve themselves. Pasta is a convivial, sharing food; to our mind, it is best not formally plated.

We leave the last word to the actor Alberto Sordi in the wonderful movie *A Taxi Driver in America* -

*Dove c'è pasta, c'è speranza.*

Where there's pasta, there's hope.

*Anna Enic*

# NOTES FROM THE COOKS

BEFORE YOU COOK read through the recipe carefully. Make sure you have all the equipment and ingredients required.

## ON COOKING TIMES

Always take cooking times as guideline rather than gospel. In each recipe, we qualify estimated cooking times with a description of how the ingredient should look at the end of cooking time, for instance "cook until soft, 5 minutes". It is better to cook the ingredient until its appearance matches the given description rather than simply setting the stopwatch.

Various factors affect cooking times, with your choice of pan and the character of your oven at the top of the list.

The size and shape of a pan directly affect how quickly a dish will cook. The same sauce cooked over the same heat will cook faster in a wide, shallow pan and more slowly in a tall, deep pot. The larger cooking surface of a wide pan ensures rapid evaporation, while the high sides of deep pots will inhibit evaporation. In each recipe, we have specified the size and shape of pan required for a quick cook or slow cook sauce.

Ovens vary from kitchen to kitchen. Most have hot spots, so be prepared to rotate dishes from top to bottom or from front to back during cooking time. An oven thermometer is a useful kitchen tool, allowing you to match your oven's temperature with the one specified in the recipe. Always allow a margin of 5-10 minutes either way for baking times.

## ON TASTING

Always taste food as you cook and before you serve. Don't be afraid to add or change flavours to suit your palate – the fun of cooking is in experimenting, improvising, creating. Ingredients differ from day to day, season to season and kitchen to kitchen. Be prepared to adjust sweetness, sharpness, spiciness, and, most important of all, salt, to your own taste.

## ON SALT AND PEPPER

Discerning seasoning makes the difference between good and great food. As a general rule, seasoning is best done towards the end of cooking. The optimum moment for a cook to judge how much salt and pepper a recipe requires is at the end of cooking time, when the flavours have blended.

## ON MEASURING

Accurate measurements are essential if you want the same good results each time you follow a recipe. We have given measurements in metric and imperial in all the recipes. Always stick to one set of measurements. Never use both in the same recipe.

Kitchen scales are the most accurate way to measure dry ingredients. We recommend using scales for all except the smallest amounts.

We also recommend using cooks' measuring spoons when following a recipe. All spoon measurements in the book are level unless otherwise stated. To measure dry ingredients with a spoon, scoop the ingredient lightly from the storage container, then level the surface with the edge of a straight-bladed knife.

We use standard level spoon measurements:
  1 tbsp - 15ml (½ floz)
  1 tsp - 5ml (⅙ floz)

To measure liquids, choose a transparent glass or plastic measuring jug. Always place the jug on a flat surface and check for accuracy at eye level when pouring in a liquid to measure.

A final and important rule of measuring - never measure ingredients over the mixing bowl!

# THE TEN COMMANDMENTS

Pasta is everyday food, yet any Italian knows that the cooking and serving of it calls for care and attention. Remember these ten golden rules for perfectly cooked pasta every time.

- Buy good quality Italian pasta.

- Use a large pot full of water.

- Salt the water with a generous hand.

- Boil the water and keep it boiling.

- Stir the pasta often - it will stick if you don't!

- Start timing when the water returns to the boil.

- Don't wander off! As they say in Italy, *gli spaghetti amano la compagnia* - spaghetti loves company.

- Drain immediately, but not too thoroughly.

- Have the sauce and a warmed bowl ready.

- Eat up! The only time people stop talking in Italy is when a bowl of pasta is placed on the table.

# PASTA IN THE KITCHEN

The key to making perfect pasta is to start with the right pot. When cooking 500g (1lb) dried pasta, the pot should hold about 5 litres (8½ pts) of water to give the pasta plenty of room to move around.

A pot made of an inexpensive, lightweight metal like aluminium is ideal, since it conducts heat evenly and is easy to lift when full of boiling water. A stockpot will also make a good pasta pot, as it is usually taller than it is wide and has two sturdy handles for lifting.

A large colander is also essential. A colander has the advantage over a sieve in that the water drains more slowly, which will prevent the cooked pasta from becoming a sticky mass. Choose a colander with feet so that the base stands well above the cooking water when it is emptied into the kitchen sink.

The type of pan used to cook a pasta sauce will directly affect the required cooking time and character of the finished sauce. The larger cooking surface of a wide frying pan ensures rapid evaporation, which is essential for a quick-cook sauce.

   A heavy-based, deep pot is best for a slow-cooked sauce. The high sides guard against over-evaporation and the heavy base prevents sticking when a long simmering time is required.

1. Tall, narrow, lightweight pasta pot with a lid
2. Long-handled wooden spoon for stirring pasta
3. Large colander with feet
4. Large frying pan for quick-cook sauces
5. Heavy-based pot with a lid for slow-cook sauces

NO COOK
## RED PESTO

**SERVES 4**

**60g (2 oz) sun-dried tomatoes in oil, drained**
**2 garlic cloves, crushed**
**2½ tbsp pine nuts, toasted**
**½ tsp crushed chilli flakes**
**5 tbsp extra virgin olive oil**
**½ - 2 tsp balsamic vinegar**
**black pepper**
**500g (1lb) dried pasta**

Place tomatoes, garlic, pine nuts, chilli flakes and oil in a food processor; pulse to a smooth paste. Add vinegar and pepper to taste. Set aside or store, see below. Cook pasta in a large pot of boiling, salted water, until firm to the bite if serving hot, or just firm to the bite if serving as a salad. Drain, reserving ½ cup pasta water. Return pasta with pesto to the warm pasta pot. Toss well to coat, adding reserved water as needed. Serve immediately or at room temperature.

**WHICH PASTA?**
Strands or shapes - spaghettini, spaghetti, penne.

**THINK AHEAD**
Make pesto up to 4 days in advance. Cover and refrigerate. If serving as a salad, dress pasta up to 8 hours ahead. Cover and store at room temperature.

**VARIATIONS**
## RED PESTO WITH ROCKET
Add 2 handfuls rocket leaves with the pesto and the drained pasta to the warm pasta pot. Finish as directed.

## RED PESTO WITH BASIL
Add 1 handful torn fresh basil with the pesto and the drained pasta to the warm pasta pot. Finish as directed.

NO COOK
# FRESH TOMATO

**SERVES 4**

**500g (1lb) dried pasta**
**6-7 ripe tomatoes, seeded and diced**
**1 garlic clove, crushed**
**5 tbsp extra virgin olive oil**
**salt, black pepper**

Cook pasta in a large pot of boiling, salted water, until firm to the bite if serving hot or just firm to the bite if serving as a salad. While pasta is cooking, combine tomatoes, garlic and oil. Add salt and pepper to taste. Let stand while pasta is cooking to allow the flavours to blend. Drain pasta. Toss drained pasta with marinated tomatoes in a large serving bowl. Serve warm or at room temperature.

**WHICH PASTA?**
Strands or thin ribbons - spaghetti, linguine.

**THINK AHEAD**
Make sauce up to 8 hours in advance. Cover and store at room temperature. If serving as a salad, dress pasta up to 8 hours in advance. Cover and store at room temperature.

**VARIATIONS**

## FRESH TOMATO AND MOZZARELLA
Return drained pasta with tomatoes and 250g (8oz) diced mozzarella to warm pasta pot. Toss well to coat. Serve immediately.

## FRESH TOMATO AND LEMON
Add 1 tbsp fresh lemon juice and ½ tsp grated lemon zest to the tomatoes. Finish as directed.

## FRESH TOMATO, RED ONION AND BASIL
Add ½ finely sliced red onion and 1 handful torn fresh basil to the tomatoes. Finish as directed.

## FRESH TOMATO AND OLIVES
Add 10 sliced pitted black olives to the tomatoes. Finish as directed.

## FRESH TOMATO, ROCKET AND BALSAMIC VINEGAR
Add 2 tsp balsamic vinegar and 1 handful roughly chopped rocket to the tomatoes, garlic and olive oil. Finish as directed.

NO COOK
# SUN-DRIED TOMATO WITH CHILLI, GARLIC AND BLACK OLIVES

**SERVES 4**

**500g (1lb) dried pasta**
**12 sun-dried tomatoes in olive oil, drained and sliced**
**150g (5oz) pitted black olives, sliced**
**3 garlic cloves, finely chopped**
**½ tsp crushed chilli flakes**
**1 tsp red wine vinegar**
**6 tbsp extra virgin olive oil**
**1 tbsp chopped fresh basil or flat-leaf parsley**
**salt, black pepper**

Cook pasta in a large pot of boiling, salted water, until firm to the bite if serving hot or just firm to the bite if serving as a salad. While pasta is cooking, combine tomatoes, olives, garlic, chilli, vinegar and oil. Drain pasta. Return pasta with basil or parsley and tomato mixture to the warm pasta pot. Toss well to coat. Add salt and pepper to taste. Serve immediately or at room temperature.

**WHICH PASTA?**
Strands or thin ribbons - spaghetti, linguine.

**THINK AHEAD**
Mix sauce ingredients up to 8 hours in advance. Cover and store at room temperature. If serving as a salad, dress pasta up to 8 hours in advance. Cover and store at room temperature.

QUICK COOK
# PUTTANESCA
**SERVES 4**

**500g (1lb) dried pasta**
**5 tbsp extra virgin olive oil**
**½ tsp crushed chilli flakes**
**2 garlic cloves, finely sliced**
**6 anchovy fillets, drained**
  **and chopped**

**2 - 400g (14oz) tins Italian**
  **plum tomatoes or 1kg (2lb)**
  **fresh tomatoes, chopped**
**150g (5oz) pitted black**
  **olives**
**1 tbsp capers, drained**
**salt, black pepper**

Cook pasta in a large pot of boiling, salted water, until firm to the bite. While pasta is cooking, heat oil in a large frying pan. Add chilli flakes, garlic and anchovies. Cook, stirring constantly over medium heat, until anchovies have disintegrated,

2-3 minutes. Raise heat to medium high, add tomatoes and cook, stirring occasionally, until thickened, 15 minutes. Add olives and capers. Add salt and pepper to taste. Drain pasta. Add drained pasta to the hot sauce and toss well to coat. Serve immediately.

**WHICH PASTA?**
Strands or tubes - spaghetti, penne, rigatoni.

**THINK AHEAD**
Make sauce up to 3 days in advance. Cover and refrigerate.

**COOKS' NOTE**
The name derives from 'puttana' - prostitute. It allegedly originated in Trastevere, the haunt in Rome of these nocturnal ladies. And its name no doubt owes something to the fact that it is a piquant sauce, very quickly made.

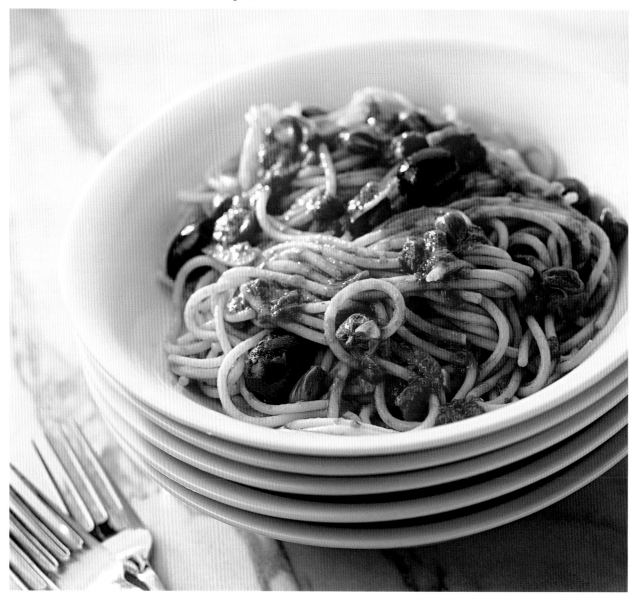

QUICK COOK
# NAPOLITANA

**SERVES 4**

**500g (1lb) dried pasta**
**7 tbsp extra virgin olive oil**
**1 garlic clove, crushed**
**1kg (2lb) fresh ripe tomatoes,**
  **chopped or 2 - 400g (14oz) tin**
  **Italian plum tomatoes, chopped**
**1 tsp sugar**
**1 handful torn fresh basil**
**salt, black pepper**

Cook pasta in a large pot of boiling, salted water until firm to the bite. While pasta is cooking, place oil, garlic, sugar, tomatoes and basil in a large frying pan on medium-high heat. Simmer rapidly until thickened, 10 minutes. Add salt and pepper to taste. Drain pasta. Add pasta to the hot sauce. Toss well to coat. Serve immediately.

**WHICH PASTA?**
Strands or tubes - spaghetti, penne, rigatoni.

**THINK AHEAD**
Make sauce up to 3 days in advance. Cover and refrigerate.

QUICK COOK
# ARRABBIATA

**SERVES 4**

**7 tbsp extra virgin olive oil**
**1 medium onion, finely sliced**
**3 garlic cloves, sliced**
**1 tsp crushed chilli flakes**
**2 - 400g (14oz) tins Italian plum**
  **tomatoes, chopped**
**salt, black pepper**
**500g (1lb) dried pasta**
**2 tbsp torn fresh basil or flat-leaf**
  **parsley, optional**

Heat oil in a large frying pan. Add onion, garlic and chilli and cook, stirring frequently over medium high heat, until soft and golden, 7 minutes. Add tomatoes and cook, stirring occasionally, until thickened, 15 minutes. Add salt and pepper to taste. Meanwhile, cook pasta in a large pot of boiling, salted water until firm to the bite. Drain. Add pasta with your choice of herb, if using, to the hot sauce. Toss to coat. Serve immediately.

**WHICH PASTA?**
Strands or tubes - spaghetti, penne, rigatoni.

**THINK AHEAD**
Make sauce up to 3 days in advance. Cover and refrigerate.

**COOKS' NOTE**
The name of this sauce from Central Italy means 'angry', because of the potency of its flavour.

QUICK COOK
# FRESH TOMATO SAUCE

**SERVES 4**

**500g (1lb) dried pasta**
**6 tbsp extra virgin olive oil**
**3 garlic cloves, crushed**
**750g (1½ lb) ripe fresh**
**  tomatoes, peeled (optional)**
**  and cut into 6 pieces**

**salt, black pepper**
**1 handful torn fresh basil**
**  leaves, optional**
**additional extra virgin**
**  olive oil to toss**

Cook pasta in a large pot of boiling, salted water, until firm to the bite. While pasta is cooking, heat oil in a large frying pan. Add garlic and cook over medium heat until fragrant, 1 minute. Add tomatoes and cook, stirring frequently, until tomatoes are sizzling hot but still retaining their fresh flavour and bright colour, about 5 minutes. Add salt and pepper to taste. Drain pasta. Add pasta, with the basil if using, to the hot sauce. Toss well to coat, adding 2 tbsp additional olive oil as needed. Serve immediately.

**WHICH PASTA?**
Strands or thin to medium ribbons - spaghetti, fettuccine, tagliatelle.

**VARIATIONS**
## FRESH TOMATO SAUCE WITH PESTO
Omit basil. Add 3 tbsp simple basil pesto (see page 105) with the drained pasta to the hot sauce.

## FRESH TOMATO SAUCE WITH MOLTEN MOZZARELLA
Make sauce as directed. Turn down heat to low. Add 125g (4oz) diced mozzarella to sauce and heat gently until just melting, for 1 minute. Omit the additional 2 tbsp olive oil. Finish as directed.

## PIQUANT FRESH TOMATO SAUCE
Add 8 sliced pitted black olives, 2 tsp capers, rinsed and drained, and ¼ tsp crushed chilli flakes with the tomatoes to the pan. Finish as directed.

## FRESH TOMATO SAUCE WITH RICOTTA
Make sauce as directed. Turn down heat to low. Add 125g (4oz) crumbled ricotta to sauce and heat gently until warm through, 1 minute. Omit the additional 2 tbsp olive oil. Finish as directed.

## SPICY FRESH TOMATO SAUCE
Add ¼ tsp crushed chilli flakes with the garlic to the pan. Finish as directed.

SLOW COOK
# TOMATO AND MOZZARELLA AL FORNO

**SERVES 4**

**2 tbsp extra virgin olive oil**

**2 cloves garlic, crushed**

**2 - 400g (14oz) tins Italian plum tomatoes, chopped or 1kg (2lb) fresh tomatoes, seeded and chopped**

**2 tsp fresh or 1 tsp dried oregano**

**salt, black pepper**

**500g (1lb) dried pasta**

**250g (8oz) mozzarella cheese, cut in to 2.5cm (1in) cubes**

**60g (2oz) freshly grated parmesan, plus additional to serve**

Preheat oven to 200°C (400°F) Gas 6.

Heat oil in a large frying pan. Add garlic and cook over medium high heat until fragrant, 1 minute. Add tomatoes and oregano and simmer rapidly, stirring occasionally, until thickened, 15 minutes. Add salt and pepper to taste. Remove and reserve 6 tbsp tomato sauce from the pan. Meanwhile, cook pasta in a large pot of boiling, salted water, until just firm to the bite. Drain, reserving ½ cup pasta water. Toss drained pasta with remaining sauce, adding reserved water as needed. Place half the pasta in an oiled 30cm x 20cm x 5cm (12in x 8in x 3in) oven-proof dish. Cover with half the mozzarella and half the parmesan. Top with remaining pasta. Cover with reserved tomato sauce and remaining mozzarella. Sprinkle with remaining parmesan. Bake until golden and bubbling, 15 minutes.

### WHICH PASTA?
Tubes or shapes - penne, rigatoni, fusilli.

### THINK AHEAD
Assemble and leave to cool completely. Cover unbaked and refrigerate up to 8 hours in advance. Bake as directed. Alternatively, cover unbaked and freeze up to 3 weeks in advance. Defrost overnight in refrigerator. Cook in preheated 200°C (400°F) Gas 6 oven for 30 minutes.

### VARIATION
## PAN-COOKED TOMATO AND MOZZARELLA
Make sauce as directed, but over low heat add mozzarella to the hot sauce and heat gently until just melting, 1 minute. Meanwhile, cook pasta in a large pot of boiling, salted water, until firm to the bite. Drain, reserving ½ cup pasta water. Add drained pasta with parmesan to the hot sauce. Toss well to coat, adding reserved water as needed. Serve hot with extra parmesan.

### SLOW COOK
## ROAST TOMATO

**SERVES 4**

**6 fresh ripe tomatoes, halved**
**2 garlic cloves, crushed**
**¼ tsp crushed chilli flakes**
**½ tsp dried oregano**
**salt, black pepper**
**3 tbsp extra virgin olive oil**
**2 tbsp balsamic vinegar**
**500g (1lb) dried pasta**
**2 tbsp freshly grated parmesan,**
  **plus additional to serve**
**additional extra virgin olive oil**

Preheat oven to 150°C (300°F) Gas 2.
Place tomato halves cut side up in an
oven tray. Sprinkle with garlic, chilli
flakes, oregano, salt and pepper. Drizzle
over oil and vinegar. Roast in oven
until very soft and wilted, 1½ hours.
Meanwhile, cook pasta in a large pot
of boiling, salted water, until firm to
the bite. Drain. Place drained pasta in
a warm bowl and toss with parmesan
and 1-2 tbsp additional extra virgin
olive oil. Place tomatoes on top. Serve
immediately with additional parmesan.

**WHICH PASTA?**
Strands or ribbons – spaghetti, linguine, fettuccine,
tagliatelle, pappardelle.

**THINK AHEAD**
Roast tomatoes up to 1 day in advance. Cover
and refrigerate. Reheat in preheated 200°C (400°F)
Gas 6 oven for 10 minutes.

**VARIATIONS**
## ROAST TOMATO WITH PESTO

Add 4 tbsp simple basil pesto (see page
105) in place of the parmesan and oil to
the drained pasta.

## ROAST TOMATO WITH RICOTTA AND BASIL

Add 125g (4oz) crumbled ricotta and
1 handful torn basil with the parmesan to
the drained pasta.

## ROAST TOMATO WITH CRISPY PANCETTA

Cook 4 unsmoked pancetta or unsmoked
streaky bacon slices, turning frequently,
in a large frying pan over medium low
heat until browned and crisp, 10 minutes.
Drain on paper towels and cut into strips
2.5cm (1in) wide. Add pancetta with the
parmesan to the drained pasta.

SLOW COOK
# SIMMERED TOMATO

**SERVES 4**

**4 tbsp extra virgin olive oil**
**1 medium onion, finely chopped**
**1 garlic clove, crushed**
**2 - 400g (14oz) tin plum tomatoes, chopped**
**salt, black pepper**
**500g (1lb) dried pasta**
**freshly grated parmesan to serve, optional**

Place oil, onion, garlic and tomatoes in a heavy based pot. Bring to a fast simmer over medium heat. Turn heat to low and simmer gently, stirring occasionally, until thick and deep red, 30-40 minutes. If the sauce becomes too dry and starts to stick, add a few tablespoons of water. Add salt and pepper to taste. Meanwhile, cook pasta in a large pot of boiling, salted water, until firm to the bite. Drain. Add pasta to the hot sauce. Toss well to coat. Serve immediately with parmesan.

**WHICH PASTA?**
Strands and tubes - spaghettini, spaghetti, penne, rigatoni.

**THINK AHEAD**
Make up to 3 days in advance. Cover and refrigerate. If making variations with cream, add cream just before serving.

VARIATIONS
## SIMMERED TOMATO WITH
## RED WINE AND ROSEMARY
Add 125ml (4floz) red wine and 2 tsp finely chopped fresh rosemary with the onion, garlic and tomatoes to the pot. Cook and serve as directed.

## SIMMERED TOMATO WITH AROMATICS
Add 1 finely chopped celery stalk and 1 finely chopped small carrot with the onion, garlic and tomatoes to the pan. Cook and serve as directed.

## SIMMERED TOMATO WITH CINNAMON AND BAY
Add ¼ tsp cinnamon and 5 dry or 10 fresh bay leaves with the onion, garlic and tomatoes to the pan. Cook and serve as directed, removing the bay leaves before serving.

## SIMMERED TOMATO WITH CREAM
Omit oil. Cook sauce as directed. Transfer to food processor; pulse until smooth. Return to pan over medium heat. Stir in 125ml (4floz) double cream and cook until hot through, 1-2 minutes. Serve as directed.

## SIMMERED TOMATO WITH VODKA
Omit oil. Cook sauce as directed. Transfer to food processor; pulse until smooth. Return to pan over medium heat. Add 3 tbsp vodka and simmer rapidly to evaporate alcohol, 2 minutes. Stir in 125ml (4floz) double cream and 30g (1oz) butter and cook until hot through, 1-2 minutes. Serve as directed.

# PASTA WITH BUTTER AND CHEESE

# CHEESE IN THE PASTA PANTRY

No pasta lover's pantry is complete without a wedge of Parmesan in the refrigerator. Always buy Parmesan in a piece, never pre-grated. It's best to buy a wedge that weighs no more than 250g-300g (8-10oz), as a larger piece will probably dry out before you use it up. Store wrapped in foil in the warmest part of the refrigerator. If it does dry out, try wrapping it in a piece of damp muslin to re-moisten. Parmesan can be frozen and it will retain its flavour well, but it will become too crumbly to grate when defrosted.

We always buy Italian Parmesan and, whenever possible, *Parmigiano Reggiano*. Although more expensive, it is unquestionably superior in flavour and texture. We like to present Parmesan at the table in a manageable piece with a small hand grater and allow everyone to enjoy freshly grating their own additional cheese. Otherwise, grate it first in the kitchen and serve it in a bowl.

*Pecorino Romano* is a tangy, salty sheep's milk cheese which is also suitable for grating. It is traditionally served with pasta dishes originating from southern Italy, where pungent flavours dominate. When called for in a recipe, it is because the distinctively sharp taste of Pecorino is the best complement to the sauce. And, although we do list grated Parmesan as an alternative, we urge you to seek out Pecorino cheese from Italian speciality and gourmet shops to serve when it is the appropriate choice for the recipe.

Gorgonzola is a creamy coloured, blue-veined cheese with a flavour that varies from mildly tangy to piquant. When buying Gorgonzola for pasta, remember that the creamier the consistency, the mellower the flavour.

When buying mozzarella at the supermarket, always choose whole milk "fresh" mozzarella that comes in a squashed, ball shape and is sold in plastic bags surrounded by water. Never buy the rubbery blocks of mozzarella. Real mozzarella is made from the milk of the Italian water buffalo and has a fresher flavour than mozzarella made from cow's milk. But, for cooking, the superior buffalo mozzarella is not essential.

NO COOK
# BUTTER AND PARMESAN

**SERVES 4**

**500g (1lb) dried pasta**
**125g (4oz) butter, cut into cubes**
**100g (3½ oz) freshly grated parmesan**
**salt, black pepper**
**additional freshly grated parmesan, to serve**

Cook pasta in a large pot of boiling, salted water, until firm to the bite. Drain. Return pasta to the warm pasta pot. Add butter to the pasta. Toss well to coat. Add parmesan and salt and pepper to taste. Serve immediately with additional parmesan.

**WHICH PASTA?**
Strands or ribbons - spaghetti, tagliolini, fettuccine, tagliatelle, pappardelle.

**COOKS' NOTE**
Don't hold back on the black pepper - this dish is best with generous amounts.

VARIATIONS
## BUTTER, PARMESAN AND HAM
Add 4 slices ham, cut into short, fine strips, 2.5cm (1in) long and 0.5cm (¼ in) wide, to pasta with butter. Finish as directed.

## BUTTER, PARMESAN AND PARSLEY
Add 2 tbsp finely chopped fresh flat-leaf parsley to pasta with the butter. Finish as directed.

## BUTTER, PARMESAN AND ASPARAGUS
Cook 250g (8oz) small asparagus tips in boiling, salted water until just tender, 2-3 minutes. Drain and add immediately to hot pasta with the butter. Toss gently to avoid crushing. Finish as directed.

## BUTTER, PARMESAN AND PEAS
Cook 125g (4oz) tiny frozen peas in boiling, salted water until just tender, 2 minutes. Drain and add immediately to hot pasta with the butter. Finish as directed.

# PASTA WITH SEAFOOD

## SMOKED SALMON, VODKA AND DILL

SERVES 4

**500g (1lb) dried pasta**
**60g (2oz) butter**
**1 tsp vodka**
**125ml (4floz) sour cream**
**salt, black pepper**
**200g (7oz) smoked salmon,**
  **cut into strips**
**1 tbsp dill sprigs**

Cook pasta in a large pot of boiling, salted water, until firm to the bite. Drain, reserving ½ cup pasta water. Return drained pasta to the warm pasta pot. Add butter, vodka and half the sour cream. Toss well to coat, adding reserved water as needed. Add salt and pepper to taste. Top with salmon, remaining sour cream and dill. Serve immediately.

**WHICH PASTA?**
Thin to medium ribbons - linguine, fettuccine, tagliatelle.

## TUNA WITH LEMON AND CAPERS

SERVES 4

**500g (1lb) dried pasta**
**2 – 200g (7oz) tins tuna in oil,**
  **drained and flaked**
**250g (8oz) cherry tomatoes**
**1 tbsp drained capers**
**handful fresh basil, torn**
**6 tbsp extra virgin olive oil**
**½ tsp lemon zest**
**2 tbsp lemon juice**
**salt, black pepper**

Cook pasta in a large pot of boiling, salted water, until firm to the bite if serving hot or just firm to the bite if serving as a salad. Drain. Return drained pasta to the warm pasta pot. Add tuna, tomatoes, capers, basil, oil and lemon zest and juice. Toss well to coat. Add salt and pepper to taste. Serve immediately or at room temperature.

**WHICH PASTA**
Tubes or shells - conchiglie, gnocchi, rigatoni.
**THINK AHEAD**
Make up to 1 day in advance if serving as a pasta salad. Cover and refrigerate. Bring to room temperature before serving.

## SALMON CAVIAR WITH BUTTER AND CHIVES

**SERVES 4**

**500g (1lb) dried pasta**
**90g (3oz) butter**
**2 tbsp finely chopped chives**
**100g (3½ oz) salmon caviar**
**salt, black pepper**

Cook pasta in a large pot of boiling, salted water, until firm to the bite. Drain, reserving about ½ cup pasta water. Return pasta with butter and chives to the warm pasta pot. Toss well to coat, adding reserved water as needed. Add caviar and toss carefully to avoid crushing caviar. Add salt and pepper to taste. Serve immediately.

**WHICH PASTA?**
Thin strands - capellini, spaghettini, paglia e fieno.

**COOKS' NOTE**
If using capellini or paglia e fieno - called straw and hay - be sure to cook in plenty of boiling water. Stir with a long wooden fork as soon as the pasta is in the water, and drain when pasta is still slightly undercooked.

## PRAWNS WITH LEMON AND BASIL

**SERVES 4**

**500g (1lb) dried pasta**
**350g (12oz) cooked, peeled large prawns**
**2 garlic cloves, finely chopped**
**½ red onion, finely chopped**
**½ tsp crushed chilli flakes**
**2 tbsp lemon juice**
**5 tbsp extra virgin olive oil**
**12 cherry tomatoes, halved**
**2 tbsp chopped fresh basil**
**salt, black pepper**

Cook pasta in a large pot of boiling, salted water, until firm to the bite if serving hot or just firm to the bite if serving as a salad. While pasta is cooking, combine prawns, garlic, onion, chilli flakes, lemon juice, oil, tomatoes and basil in a bowl. Drain pasta. Return pasta with prawn and tomato mixture to the warm pasta pot. Toss well to coat. Add salt and pepper to taste. Serve immediately or at room temperature.

**WHICH PASTA?**
Thin strands or medium shells - spaghetti, gnocchi, conchiglie.

**THINK AHEAD**
Make up to 8 hours in advance if serving as a salad. Cover and refrigerate. Return to room temperature before serving.

**COOKS' NOTE**
For the most authentic Italian flavour, use a peppery olive oil such as Tuscan or Umbrian.

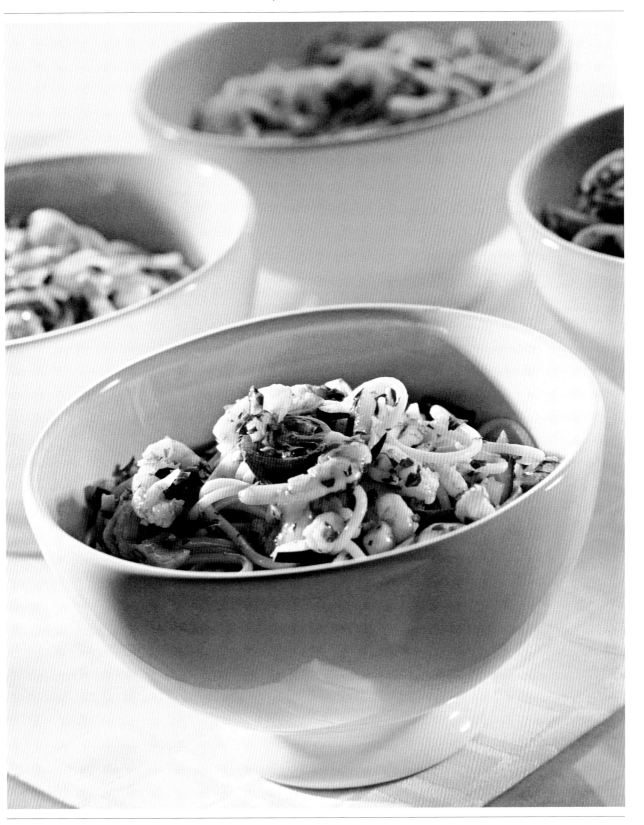

QUICK COOK
# SCALLOPS WITH GARLIC AND CRISP CRUMBS

**SERVES 4**

**500g (1lb) dried pasta**
**8 tbsp extra virgin olive oil**
**2 garlic cloves, finely chopped**
**2 tbsp chopped fresh flat-leaf parsley**
**60g (2oz) dried breadcrumbs (see page 160)**
**½ tsp crushed chilli flakes**
**12 scallops, cut into quarters, or 24 queen scallops**
**salt, black pepper**

Cook pasta in a large pot of boiling, salted water, until firm to the bite. While pasta is cooking, heat oil in a large frying pan. Add garlic, parsley, breadcrumbs and chilli flakes and cook over a high heat, 1 minute. Add scallops and cook, stirring constantly, until just turning opaque, 1-2 minutes. Add salt and pepper to taste. Drain pasta and add to hot pan. Toss well to coat. Serve immediately.

**WHICH PASTA?**
Thin to medium ribbons - linguine, fettuccine.

**COOKS' NOTE**
Timing is everything in this sauce. The pasta must be ready when the scallops are ready. Scallops become tough if overcooked. A sweet olive oil, preferably Ligurian, will best complement the scallops' natural sweetness.

QUICK COOK
# WHITE CLAMS

**SERVES 4**

**1kg (2lb) small clams, in shells**
**125ml (4floz) dry white wine**
**500g (1lb) dried pasta**
**4 tbsp extra virgin olive oil**
**¼ tsp crushed chilli flakes**

**2 garlic cloves, finely chopped**
**2 tbsp finely chopped fresh flat-leaf parsley**
**additional 2 tbsp extra virgin olive oil**
**salt, black pepper**

Scrub clams under running water. Discard any that are broken or not tightly closed. Place clams with wine in a large pot with a lid on. Steam over medium heat until shells are open, shaking pot occasionally to ensure even cooking, about 4-5 minutes. Use a slotted spoon to lift out clams, and set aside. Discard any that do not open. Tip the pot and slowly pour out the clear clam and wine juices, taking care to leave the sandy residue in the pot. Reserve juices and discard residue. Remove clams from shells and reserve, discarding shells.
Cook pasta in large pot of boiling, salted water, until firm to the bite. While pasta is cooking, heat oil in a large frying pan. Add chilli flakes, garlic and parsley. Cook over medium heat until fragrant, 1 minute. Add reserved clam juices and boil vigorously for 1 minute. Remove from heat.
Drain pasta. Add pasta to hot clam juices. Return to heat and cook, tossing constantly, for 1 minute. Add clams and 2 tbsp olive oil and toss well to coat. Add salt and pepper to taste. Serve immediately.

**WHICH PASTA?**
Strands or thin ribbons – spaghettini, spaghetti, linguine.

**COOKS' NOTE**
A simple variation for this recipe is to replace clams with mussels. Cook as directed above. You could leave a handful of mussels in their bottom shells as a garnish.

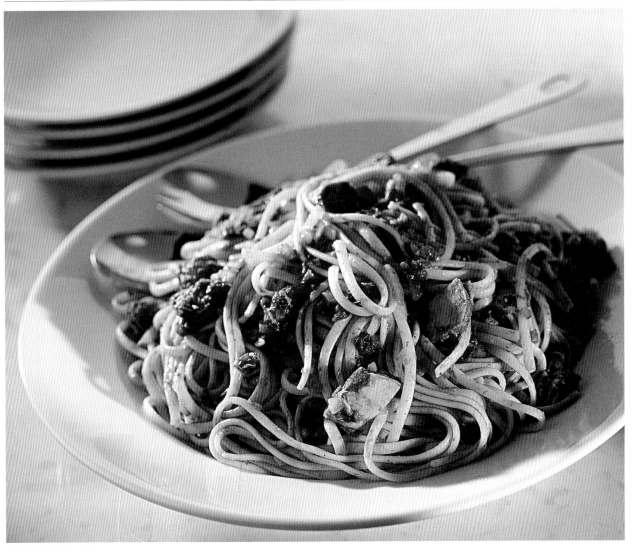

# TUNA AND TOMATO
SERVES 4

**6 tbsp extra virgin olive oil**
**1 small onion, finely chopped**
**2 garlic cloves, crushed**
**1 - 400g (14oz) tin Italian plum tomatoes, chopped**
**1 - 200g (7oz) tin tuna in oil, drained and flaked**
**salt, black pepper**
**500g (1lb) dried pasta**

Heat oil in a large frying pan. Add onion and garlic and cook,
stirring constantly over medium high heat, until softened,
5 minutes. Add tomatoes. Simmer rapidly until just thickened,
10 minutes. Add tuna and cook until hot through, 3 minutes.
Add salt and pepper to taste. Meanwhile, cook pasta in a large
pot of boiling, salted water, until firm to the bite. Drain. Add
pasta to the hot sauce. Toss well to coat. Serve immediately.

**WHICH PASTA?**
Strands, thin ribbons or tubes - spaghetti, linguine or penne.

**THINK AHEAD**
Make sauce up to 2 days in advance. Cover and refrigerate.

**VARIATION**
## PIQUANT TUNA WITH TOMATOES
Add 1 tbsp rinsed capers and 12 sliced pitted black olives to
the pan with the tuna. Finish as directed.

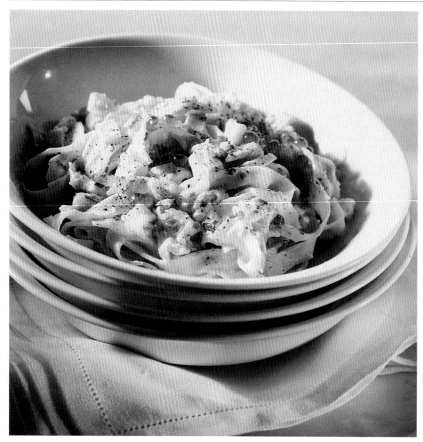

## CHILLI SQUID

**SERVES 4**

**500g (1lb) dried pasta**
**5 tbsp extra virgin olive oil**
**4 garlic cloves, finely sliced**
**½ tsp crushed chilli flakes**
**350g (12oz) squid, cleaned and cut into 1cm (½ in) rings**
**2 tbsp lemon juice**
**2 tbsp finely chopped fresh flat-leaf parsley**
**salt, black pepper**

Cook pasta in a large pot of boiling, salted water, until firm to the bite. While pasta is cooking, heat oil in a large frying pan. Add garlic and chilli and cook over high heat until just golden, 1-2 minutes. Add squid and cook, stirring constantly, until opaque, 2-3 minutes. Add lemon juice, parsley and salt and pepper to taste. Drain pasta. Add pasta to the hot squid. Toss well to coat. Serve immediately.

**WHICH PASTA?**
Strands or thin ribbons - spaghetti, linguine.

**COOKS' NOTE**
Squid needs to be cooked either quickly over high heat or slowly over low heat to avoid a tough, rubbery texture. In this recipe, be sure to combine with the pasta as soon as the squid is cooked.

**VARIATION**
## CHILLI PRAWNS
Replace squid with 350g (12oz) large raw peeled prawns. Cook as directed until prawns are pink and firm, 3-4 minutes. Finish as directed.

## SMOKED SALMON WITH WHITE WINE, CREAM AND CHIVES

**SERVES 4**

**60g (2oz) butter**
**2 shallots, finely chopped**
**200ml (7floz) white wine**
**175ml (6floz) double cream**
**grated zest of ½ lemon**
**2 tbsp lemon juice**

**2 tbsp chopped fresh chives**
**200g (7oz) smoked salmon slices, cut into strips**
**salt, black pepper**
**500g (1lb) dried pasta**
**4 tsp salmon roe, optional**

Melt butter in a large frying pan over medium-low heat. Add shallots and cook, stirring occasionally, until soft, 5 minutes. Add wine and simmer until reduced by half, 3 minutes. Add cream, lemon zest and juice, chives and salmon. Heat over medium-low heat, without boiling, until hot through, 1 minute. Add salt and pepper to taste. Meanwhile, cook pasta in a large pot of boiling, salted water, until firm to the bite. Drain, reserving ½ cup pasta water. Add pasta to the hot sauce. Toss well to coat, adding reserved water as needed. Top with salmon roe, if using. Serve immediately.

**WHICH PASTA?**
Thin to medium ribbons - tagliolini, fettuccine, tagliatelle.

QUICK COOK
## SCALLOPS WITH CREME FRAICHE AND DILL

SERVES 4

**500g (1lb) dried pasta**
**60g (2oz) butter**
**6 spring onions, finely sliced**
**8 scallops, cut into quarters**
**3 tbsp crème fraîche**
**2 tbsp chopped fresh dill**
**salt, black pepper**

Cook pasta in a large pot of boiling, salted water, until firm to the bite. While pasta is cooking, melt butter in a large frying pan over medium heat. Add spring onions and cook, stirring frequently, until soft, 3 minutes. Add scallops and cook, stirring constantly, until just turning opaque, 1-2 minutes. Add crème fraîche and dill. Continue cooking until heated through, 1 minute. Drain pasta, reserving ½ cup pasta water. Add pasta to hot sauce. Toss well to coat, adding reserved water as needed. Add salt and pepper to taste. Serve immediately.

**WHICH PASTA?**
Thin to medium ribbons - linguine, tagliolini, fettuccine, tagliatelle.

QUICK COOK
## SPICY GARLIC PRAWNS WITH CHERRY TOMATOES

**SERVES 4**

**500g (1lb) dried pasta**
**5 tbsp extra virgin olive oil**
**½ tsp crushed chilli flakes**
**4 garlic cloves, finely chopped**
**500g (1lb) large raw prawns in shells**
**250g (8oz) cherry tomatoes, halved**
**salt, black pepper**
**2 tbsp chopped fresh flat-leaf parsley**

Cook pasta in a large pot of boiling, salted water, until just firm to the bite. Heat oil in a large frying pan. Add chilli and garlic and cook over high heat until pale gold, 1 minute. Add prawns and cook, stirring constantly, until just turning pink, 1 minute. Add tomatoes and cook, stirring constantly, until tomatoes are hot and wilted and prawns are firm, 2-3 minutes. Add salt and pepper to taste. Drain pasta. Add drained pasta with parsley to hot sauce. Toss well to coat. Serve immediately.

**WHICH PASTA?**
Strands and thin ribbons - spaghettini, spaghetti, linguine.

**VARIATION**
## SPICY GARLIC SCALLOPS
Replace prawns with 350g (12oz) scallops, halved. Cook as directed until just opaque, 2-3 minutes. Finish as directed.

SLOW COOK
# RED MUSSELS

SERVES 4

FOR TOMATO SAUCE
**4 tbsp extra virgin olive oil**
**2 garlic cloves, finely chopped**
**¼ tsp crushed chilli flakes**
**1 - 400g (14oz) tin Italian plum tomatoes, chopped, or**
  **500g (1lb) fresh ripe tomatoes, peeled and chopped**
**salt, black pepper**

**1kg (2lb) mussels**
**5 tbsp white wine**
**500g (1lb) dried pasta**
**2 tbsp fresh flat-leaf parsley, chopped**

Heat oil in a large frying pan. Add garlic and chilli and cook
over medium-high heat until just golden, 6 minutes. Add
tomatoes. Simmer rapidly, stirring occasionally, until thick,
15 minutes. Add salt and pepper to taste.
Meanwhile, scrub mussels under running water. Discard any
that are broken or not tightly closed. Place mussels and wine
in a large pot with a lid on. Steam over medium heat, shaking
occasionally, until shells are open, 4-5 minutes. Remove
mussels with a slotted spoon and set aside. Discard any that
do not open. Tip the pot and slowly pour out the clear mussel
juices, taking care to leave the sandy residue in the pot.
Reserve juices and discard residue.
Meanwhile, cook pasta in a large pot of boiling, salted water,
until firm to the bite. Drain pasta and add with mussels,
mussel juices and parsley to the hot sauce. Toss gently.
Serve immediately.

WHICH PASTA?
Strands or thin ribbons - spaghettini, spaghetti, linguine.

THINK AHEAD
Make tomato sauce up to 3 days in advance. Cover and refrigerate. Reheat
before combining with mussels and pasta as directed.

COOKS' NOTE
For a more elegant presentation, remove and discard the empty half of the
mussel shells.

VARIATION
## RED CLAMS
Replace mussels with 1kg (2lb) small clams in shells.
Cook as directed.

SLOW COOK
# SEAFOOD EXTRAVAGANZA
SERVES 4 - 6

**500g (1lb) mussels or small clams in shells**
**125ml (4floz) white wine**
**5 tbsp extra virgin olive oil**
**4 garlic cloves, crushed**
**8 large raw prawns with shells**
**4 medium squid, cleaned and cut**
 **into 1cm (½ in) rings**
**4 cooked langoustines**
**1 fresh red chilli, finely sliced**
**4 medium tomatoes, peeled, seeded**
 **and diced (see pages 156 & 158)**
**salt, black pepper**
**500g (1lb) dried pasta**
**1 handful whole fresh basil leaves**
**additional extra virgin olive oil for drizzling**

Scrub mussels or clams under running water. Discard any that are broken or not tightly closed. Place wine and mussels or clams in a large, heavy based pot with a lid over medium-high heat. Cook, shaking pan frequently, until shells open, 4-5 minutes. Remove mussels or clams with a slotted spoon and reserve. Discard any that do not open. Tip pot and slowly pour out clear seafood juices, taking care to leave sandy residue in the pot. Reserve juices and discard residue. Rinse pot.

Heat oil in the pot over high heat. Add garlic and prawns and cook, stirring constantly, until the prawns are just turning pink, 2 minutes. Add the squid, langoustine, chilli and tomatoes. Cook, stirring constantly, until the squid is just opaque, 3-4 minutes. Add reserved seafood juices and heat through, 30 seconds. Add salt and pepper to taste. Remove from heat.

Meanwhile, cook pasta in a large pot of boiling, salted water, until firm to the bite. Drain. Add pasta with basil to the hot sauce. Toss gently to coat. Drizzle over about 1-2 tbsp additional olive oil. Serve immediately.

**WHICH PASTA?**
Thin strands or ribbons- spaghettini, spaghetti, or linguine.

**COOKS' NOTE**
For cooking you can use any good extra virgin oil, but for the final drizzle we suggest a peppery extra virgin oil from Puglia or from Tuscany.

# PASTA WITH MEAT

# MEAT IN THE PASTA PANTRY

Pancetta is an Italian streaky bacon, but it has a distinctly different flavour from regular streaky bacon as it is cured differently. Unsmoked streaky bacon can be used instead, but, for authentic Italian flavour, we urge you to seek out pancetta from Italian speciality or gourmet shops. Buy several pieces about 60g (2oz), each cut into 5-10mm (¼-½ in) slices. Wrap separately and store in the freezer for up to 3 months. This way you will always have the real thing on hand when it is called for.

Prosciutto is a specially cured Italian ham that comes from the hind thigh of the pig and is air-cured for over a year. This long process of air-curing gives it a distinctively sweet flavour and delicate rosy colour. Buy prosciutto sliced to order and avoid the packages of ready sliced meat wherever possible. Store it well wrapped in the refrigerator for no more than three days.

There is an old adage from Parma that says: *Grasso e magro non del tutto, ecco il pregio del prosciutto.* This means that prosciutto must have the right balance of fat and meat. When buying, look for prosciutto with a generous proportion of fat, as this contributes as much to the flavour as the meat part.

The best sausage to use for making pasta sauces is Luganega, a sweet medium-ground sausage. If you cannot find it, use a coarse-ground sausage with a very high percentage of pork meat, such as Cumberland or Toulouse, or any other mild sausage not containing herbs or garlic.

QUICK COOK
# PROSCIUTTO AND CREAM

**SERVES 4**

500g (1lb) dried pasta
60g (2oz) butter
200g (7oz) prosciutto slices, cut
  into strips 1cm (½ in) wide
½ small onion, finely chopped
4 tbsp dry white wine
125ml (4floz) double cream
salt, black pepper
4 tbsp freshly grated parmesan,
  plus additional to serve

Cook pasta in a large pot of boiling, salted water, until firm to the bite. While pasta is cooking, melt butter in a large frying pan over medium-low heat. Add prosciutto strips and onion and cook, stirring frequently, until onion is soft, 4-5 minutes. Add wine and raise heat to medium-high. Simmer until just evaporated. Add cream and cook until just thickened, 1 minute. Remove from heat and add salt and pepper to taste. Drain pasta, reserving ½ cup pasta water. Add pasta with parmesan to the hot sauce. Toss well to coat, adding reserved water as needed. Serve immediately with additional parmesan.

**WHICH PASTA?**
Medium ribbons- fettuccine, tagliatelle.

## PIZZAIOLA

**SERVES 4**

**2 tbsp extra virgin olive oil**
**300g (1¾ lb) rump steak, cut into strips 5cm (2in) long and 1cm (½ in) wide**
**1 - 400g (14oz) tin chopped Italian plum tomatoes**
**2 garlic cloves, crushed**
**2 tsp fresh oregano or 1 tsp dried oregano**
**2 tbsp capers, drained and rinsed**
**4 tbsp pitted, sliced black olives**
**500g (1lb) dried pasta**
**1 tbsp finely chopped fresh flat-leaf parsley**

Heat oil in a large frying pan. Add steak and cook over high heat until browned all over, 3 minutes. Remove from pan with slotted spoon, cover to keep warm and reserve. Reduce heat to medium high. Add tomatoes, garlic, oregano, capers and olives. Simmer rapidly, stirring occasionally, until thickened, 10 minutes. Remove pan from heat. Return steak to the pan to keep warm. Meanwhile, cook pasta in a large pot of boiling, salted water. Drain. Add pasta with parsley to the hot sauce. Toss well to coat. Serve immediately.

**WHICH PASTA?**
Strands - spaghetti, spaghettini.

**COOKS' NOTE**
This sauce is so called because it contains oregano which, with tomato, is one of the traditional ingredients for pizza.

## CRISPY PANCETTA AND SPRING ONIONS

**SERVES 4**

**8 pancetta or streaky bacon slices, smoked or unsmoked**
**30g (1oz) butter**
**2 tbsp extra virgin olive oil**
**8 spring onions, sliced**
**500g (1lb) dried pasta**
**4 tbsp freshly grated parmesan**
**salt, black pepper**
**additional freshly grated parmesan to serve**

Cook pancetta, turning frequently, in a large frying pan over medium-low heat until browned and crisp, 10 minutes. Drain on paper towels and cut into 2.5cm (1in) wide strips. Pour off excess fat from pan. Add butter and oil to pan and melt over medium heat. Add spring onions and cook, stirring constantly, until just soft, 2 minutes. Meanwhile, cook pasta in a large pot of boiling, salted water, until firm to the bite. Drain, reserving ½ cup pasta water. Add pasta with parmesan and pancetta to spring onions. Toss well to coat, adding reserved water as needed. Add salt and pepper to taste. Serve immediately with additional parmesan.

**WHICH PASTA?**
Tubes or shapes - penne, rigatoni, gnocchi, conchiglie.

**COOKS' NOTE**
Try and match the size of the pasta to the size of your ingredients. Cut the pancetta into pieces that can be easily caught in the hollow of the pasta shape.

QUICK COOK
# SAUSAGE WITH CREAM AND BASIL
SERVES 4

2 tbsp extra virgin olive oil
1 small onion, finely chopped
4 garlic cloves, crushed
250g (8oz) Italian sausages, skinned
   and crumbled

300ml (10floz) double cream
500g (1lb) dried pasta
1 handful fresh basil leaves, torn
salt, black pepper
freshly grated parmesan to serve

Heat oil in a large frying pan. Add onion and garlic and cook, stirring occasionally over medium-high heat, until just golden, 5 minutes. Add sausage and cook, stirring frequently to break up meat, until it just loses its pink colour, 10 minutes. Stir in cream and simmer until just thickened, 1-2 minutes. Add salt and pepper to taste. Meanwhile, cook pasta in a large pot of boiling, salted water, until firm to the bite. Drain, reserving ½ cup pasta water. Add pasta with basil to the hot sauce. Toss well to coat, adding reserved water as needed. Serve immediately with parmesan.

**WHICH PASTA?**
Tubes or shapes - conchiglie, fusilli, macaroni.

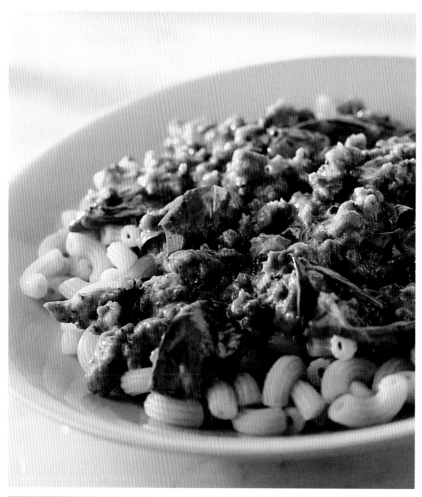

QUICK COOK
# PAN-ROAST CHICKEN WITH GARLIC AND SHALLOTS
SERVES 4-6

4 boneless chicken breasts
12 whole garlic cloves
8 whole shallots
175ml (6floz) white wine
2 tbsp extra virgin olive oil
salt, black pepper
175ml (6floz) double cream
500g (1lb) dried pasta

Preheat oven to 200°C (400°F) Gas 6.

Place chicken skin-side up, with garlic and shallots, in a large oven-proof frying pan. Pour over wine. Drizzle chicken skin with oil and sprinkle with salt and pepper. Roast until chicken is cooked through and skin is crisp and golden, 25-30 minutes. Remove chicken, garlic and shallots and cover to keep warm. Bring chicken juices to a simmer over medium high heat. Add cream and cook, stirring constantly, until hot through, 1 minute. Add salt and pepper to taste. Meanwhile, cook pasta in a large pot of boiling, salted water, until firm to the bite. Drain. Add pasta to the hot sauce. Toss well to coat. Slice each chicken breast crosswise into 3 pieces. Top pasta with chicken, garlic and shallots. Serve immediately.

**WHICH PASTA?**
Medium to wide ribbons or large tubes - tagliatelle, pappardelle, penne, rigatoni.

**COOKS' NOTE**
Snipping off the tops of the roast garlic and shallots with kitchen scissors makes it easier to squeeze out the soft, sweet cooked centres from their papery skins.

QUICK COOK
# AMATRICIANA

SERVES 4

**4 tbsp extra virgin olive oil**
**200g (7oz) unsmoked pancetta or**
**streaky bacon, cut into 0.5cm (¼ in)**
**wide strips**
**½ tsp crushed chilli flakes**
**6 tbsp dry white wine**
**1 onion, finely chopped**
**1 - 400g (14oz) tin Italian plum**
**tomatoes, chopped, or 500g (1lb)**
**fresh tomatoes, peeled and chopped**
**salt, black pepper**
**500g (1lb) dried pasta**
**4 tbsp freshly grated pecorino**
**romano or parmesan, plus**
**additional cheese to serve**

Heat oil in a large frying pan. Add
pancetta strips and chilli flakes and cook,
stirring occasionally over medium heat,
until pancetta is crisp, 5 minutes. Add
wine and simmer until reduced by half,
1 minute. Add onion and cook, stirring
frequently, until soft and just golden,
10 minutes. Turn heat to medium-high.
Add tomatoes and cook, until thickened,
10 minutes. Add salt and pepper to taste.
Meanwhile, cook pasta in a large pot of
boiling, salted water, until firm to the
bite. Drain. Add pasta with cheese to
the hot sauce. Toss well to coat. Serve
immediately with additional cheese.

**WHICH PASTA?**
Strands or tubes - spaghetti, bucatini, penne,
rigatoni.

**THINK AHEAD**
Make sauce up to 1 day in advance. Cool
completely. Cover and refrigerate.

**COOKS' NOTE**
This sauce is made in the Apennines east of Rome
for the local Festa on 15th August. The cheese
used in the traditional recipe is Pecorino, which
has the right piquancy to match the flavour of the
chilli. If you cannot find Pecorino Romano, you can
use Parmesan. The pancetta should be unsmoked.

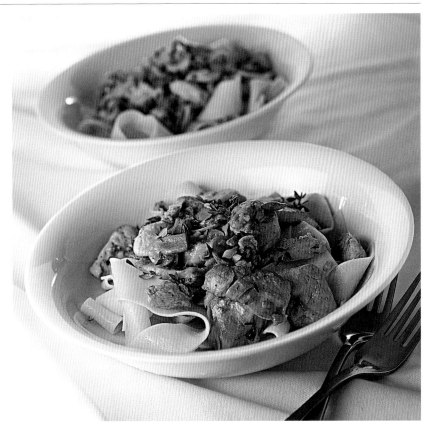

QUICK COOK
# CHICKEN WITH LEMON AND MUSHROOMS

SERVES 4

**30g (1oz) butter**
**2 skinless, boneless chicken breasts, cut across into**
**8 - 2.5 cm (1in) wide strips**
**2 garlic cloves, crushed**
**250g (8oz) brown mushrooms, sliced**
**1 tsp fresh thyme leaves**
**2 tbsp lemon juice**
**salt, black pepper**
**500g (1lb) dried pasta**
**additional 30g (1oz) butter to toss**

Melt butter in a large frying pan over medium heat. Add chicken strips and cook,
stirring frequently, until opaque, 4 minutes. Add garlic, mushrooms and thyme.
Cook, stirring frequently, until mushrooms are soft and chicken is cooked through,
4 minutes. Add lemon juice and salt and pepper to taste. Meanwhile, cook pasta in
a large pot of boiling, salted water, until firm to the bite. Drain. Add pasta to hot
sauce with additional butter. Toss well to coat. Serve immediately.

**WHICH PASTA?**
Medium to large ribbons - fettuccine, tagliatelle, pappardelle.

**THINK AHEAD**
Make sauce up to 1 day in advance. Cover and refrigerate. Reheat gently, adding 2 tbsp water.

## QUICK COOK
# VENETIAN-STYLE CHICKEN LIVER

**SERVES 4**

**250g (8oz) chicken livers**
**30g (1oz) butter**
**3 tbsp extra virgin olive oil**
**1 garlic clove, lightly crushed**
**4 fresh sage leaves**
**4 tbsp dry white wine**
**salt, black pepper**
**500g (1lb) dried pasta**
**4 tbsp freshly grated parmesan**
**15g (½ oz) additional butter to toss**
**freshly grated parmesan to serve**

Place chicken livers in sieve and rinse under cold running water. Drain and pat dry with kitchen paper. Cut each chicken liver into 3 pieces, discarding membranes and gristle. Melt butter with olive oil in a large frying pan over medium heat. Add garlic and sage and cook until garlic is golden, 2-3 minutes. Remove and discard garlic and sage. Add chicken livers and cook, stirring frequently, until browned, 1 minute. Add wine and simmer until just evaporated, 30 seconds. Add salt and pepper to taste. Meanwhile, cook pasta in a large pot of boiling, salted water, until firm to the bite. Drain. Add pasta with parmesan and additional butter to the hot sauce. Toss well to coat. Serve immediately with parmesan.

**WHICH PASTA?**
Shapes or medium to wide ribbons - conchiglie, farfalle, tagliatelle, pappardelle.

**COOKS' NOTE**
Quick cooking ensures that the chicken liver pieces will be still pink and juicy inside.

## QUICK COOK
# CARBONARA

**SERVES 4**

**3 egg yolks**
**8 tbsp freshly grated parmesan**
**2 tbsp oil**
**2 garlic cloves, peeled and halved**
**200g (7oz) unsmoked pancetta or unsmoked streaky bacon slices, cut into 0.5cm (¼ in) wide strips**
**4 tbsp white wine**
**500g (1lb) dried pasta**
**15g (½ oz) butter**
**salt, black pepper**
**additional freshly grated parmesan to serve**

Mix egg yolks and parmesan in a bowl until combined. Heat oil in a large frying pan. Add garlic and cook over medium-high heat until golden, 2 minutes. Remove garlic and discard. Add pancetta and cook, stirring occasionally, until crisp, 5 minutes. Add wine and simmer until just evaporated, 2 minutes. Remove from heat.
Meanwhile, cook pasta in a large pot of boiling, salted water, until firm to the bite. Drain, reserving ½ cup pasta water. Add drained pasta to the hot pancetta and toss well to coat. Remove from the heat. Add egg mixture and butter and toss again to coat, adding reserved water as needed. Add salt and pepper to taste. Serve immediately with additional parmesan.

**WHICH PASTA?**
Hollow or thin strands - bucatini, spaghetti.

**COOKS' NOTE**
We have sharpened the sauce with the addition of white wine. If you don't have any white wine in the pantry, use 2 tbsp dry vermouth instead.

SLOW COOK
# SPICY SAUSAGE RAGU

**SERVES 4**

3 tbsp extra virgin olive oil
1 onion, finely chopped
2 garlic cloves, finely
  chopped
250g (8oz) Italian sausages,
  skinned and crumbled
½ tsp crushed chilli flakes
1 tsp fennel seeds
1 tsp dried oregano
1 tbsp tomato purée
1 - 400g (14oz) tin chopped
  Italian plum tomatoes
150ml (5floz) double cream
salt, black pepper
500g (1lb) dried pasta
freshly grated parmesan
  to serve

Heat oil in a large frying pan. Cook
onion and garlic over medium-high heat,
stirring frequently, until soft and pale
gold, 5 minutes. Add sausage. Cook,
stirring to break up, until coloured,
10 minutes. Add chilli flakes, fennel,
oregano, tomato purée and chopped
tomatoes. Simmer, stirring occasionally,
until thickened, 20 minutes. Add cream.
Cook, stirring until heated through. Add
salt and pepper to taste.
Meanwhile, cook pasta in a large pot
of boiling, salted water, until firm to the
bite. Drain. Add pasta to the hot sauce.
Toss well to coat. Serve immediately
with parmesan.

**WHICH PASTA?**
Medium or large tubes - ditali, penne, rigatoni,
macaroni.

**THINK AHEAD**
Make ragù up to 3 days in advance. Cover and
refrigerate. Alternatively, freeze up to 1 month in
advance. Defrost overnight in refrigerator before
reheating.

**COOKS' NOTE**
If you can't find Italian sausages, use the best,
coarse-ground sausage you can buy. A good quality
Cumberland or Toulouse sausage is a reasonable
substitute.

SLOW COOK
# CLASSIC RAGU BOLOGNESE

**SERVES 4 - 6**

60g (2oz) butter
2 tbsp extra virgin olive oil
60g (2oz) unsmoked pancetta
  or unsmoked streaky bacon,
  finely chopped
1 small onion, finely chopped
1 carrot, finely chopped
1 celery stalk, finely chopped
1 garlic clove, finely chopped
1 bay leaf

500g (1lb) lean chuck steak,
  coarsely minced
2 tbsp tomato purée
150ml (5floz) red wine
150ml (5floz) meat stock,
  or water
150ml (5floz) milk
salt, black pepper, nutmeg
500g (1lb) dried pasta
freshly grated parmesan to serve

Melt butter and oil in a large, heavy-based pot over medium-high heat. Add pancetta
and cook, stirring frequently, until coloured, 5 minutes. Add onion, carrot, celery,
garlic and bay leaf and cook, stirring frequently, until soft, 8 minutes. Add minced
steak and cook, crumbling with a fork to break up, until browned. Turn heat to
medium. Add tomato purée and cook, stirring constantly, 1 minute. Add wine and
stock or water. Bring to a boil, then turn heat down to very low. Simmer, partially
covered, stirring occasionally and adding milk 2 tbsp at a time every 20-30 minutes.
Cook until thick and rich, 2 hours. Add salt, pepper and nutmeg to taste.
Meanwhile, cook pasta in a large pot of boiling, salted water until firm to the
bite. Drain. Add drained pasta to hot ragù. Toss well to coat. Serve immediately
with parmesan.

**WHICH PASTA?**
Medium ribbons or large tubes - tagliatelle, macaroni, rigatoni, penne.

**THINK AHEAD**
Make sauce up to 3 days in advance. Cover and refrigerate. Alternatively, make up to 1 month in advance
and freeze. Defrost overnight in refrigerator before reheating.

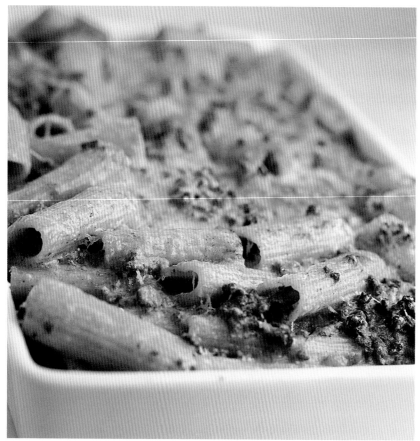

SLOW COOK
# RAGU AL FORNO
SERVES 4 - 6

500g (1lb) dried pasta
1 recipe classic ragù bolognese
  (see page 91)
3 tbsp freshly grated parmesan

FOR BECHAMEL
60g (2oz) butter
3 tbsp flour
500ml (16floz) milk
salt, pepper, nutmeg

Preheat oven to 200°C (400°F) Gas 6.
For bechamel, melt butter over medium heat in a heavy saucepan. Whisk in flour and cook until foaming, about 1 minute. Remove from heat and pour in milk gradually, whisking constantly. Return to heat and cook, whisking constantly, until sauce thickens, about 2 minutes. Bring to the boil and remove from heat. Add salt, black pepper and nutmeg to taste. Meanwhile, cook pasta in a large pot of boiling, salted water, until just firm to the bite. Drain. Toss pasta with ragù, bechamel and parmesan. Place in buttered 30cm x 20cm x 7.5cm (12in x 8in x 3in) oven-proof dish and bake until golden and crusty, 15 minutes. Leave to stand for 5 minutes before serving.

**WHICH PASTA?**
Large tubes or shells - rigatoni, penne, conchiglie.

**THINK AHEAD**
Assemble and leave cool completely. Cover, unbaked and refrigerate up to 1 day in advance. Alternatively, freeze up to 3 weeks in advance. Defrost overnight in the refrigerator.

SLOW COOK
# CHICKEN, TOMATO AND ROSEMARY RAGU
SERVES 4

FOR CHICKEN
350g (12oz) boneless, skinless
  chicken thighs
1 celery stalk, quartered
½ small onion, chopped
5 tbsp dry white wine
FOR SAUCE
5 tbsp extra virgin olive oil
1 tbsp finely chopped onion
1 tbsp finely chopped celery stalk
3 garlic cloves, finely chopped
1 tbsp finely chopped fresh flat-leaf
  parsley
1 tbsp finely chopped rosemary
grated zest of ½ lemon
1 - 400g (14oz) tin Italian plum
  tomatoes, chopped
salt, black pepper
500g (1lb) dried pasta

Place chicken, celery, onion and wine in a pan with cold water to cover. Bring slowly to a simmer over medium-low heat. Simmer gently without boiling until cooked through, 7-10 minutes. Cool completely in cooking liquid. Drain, reserving liquid, and cut chicken into 1cm (½ in) dice.
Heat oil in a large frying pan. Add onion and celery and cook, stirring occasionally, over medium-low heat until soft, 5 minutes. Add garlic, parsley and rosemary and cook until fragrant, 1 minute. Add lemon zest, tomatoes and 4 tbsp reserved poaching liquid. Reduce heat to low and simmer gently, stirring occasionally, until thick, 30 minutes. Add salt and pepper to taste. Add chicken and heat through, 3 minutes. Meanwhile, cook pasta in a large pot of boiling, salted water, until firm to the bite. Drain. Add pasta to the hot sauce. Toss well to coat. Serve immediately.

**WHICH PASTA?**
Medium tubes or shells - conchiglie, gnocchetti, macaroni.

**THINK AHEAD**
Cook chicken, but do not dice, up to 2 days in advance. Make tomato sauce up to 1 day in advance. Cover and refrigerate.

SLOW COOK
# CLASSIC LASAGNE AL FORNO
**SERVES 4**

**12 sheets dried or fresh lasagne**
**1 recipe classic ragù bolognese (see page 91)**
**6 tbsp freshly grated parmesan**

FOR BECHAMEL
**75g (2½ oz) butter**
**4½ tbsp flour**
**750ml (1¼ pints) milk**
**salt, black pepper, nutmeg**

Preheat oven to 200°C (400°F) Gas 6.

Cook pasta, 3 sheets at a time, in a large pot of boiling, salted water for half the recommended time, or until pasta is pliable but slightly hard at the centre, about 4 minutes for dried pasta, 1 minute for fresh pasta. Drain and place sheets in a single layer on tea towels.

For bechamel, melt butter over medium heat in a heavy saucepan. Whisk in flour and cook until foaming, about 1 minute. Remove from heat and pour in milk gradually, whisking constantly. Return to heat and cook, whisking constantly, until sauce thickens, about 2 minutes. Bring to the boil and remove from the heat. Add salt, pepper and nutmeg to taste.

In a buttered 30cm x 20cm x 7.5cm (12in x 8in x 3in) oven-proof dish, spread a thin layer of the bechamel. Lay 3 sheets pasta, over the bechamel. Spread a quarter of the ragù over the pasta. Spread a quarter of the bechamel over the ragù, and sprinkle with a quarter of the parmesan. Starting with another layer of 3 pasta sheets, repeat layers. Repeat layers again to finish, ending with parmesan. Bake in oven until golden and bubbling, 30 minutes. Leave to stand for 5 minutes before serving.

**WHICH PASTA?**
Egg lasagne, green or yellow, fresh when possible.

**THINK AHEAD**
Assemble lasagne and leave to cool completely. Cover, unbaked, and refrigerate up to 1 day in advance. Alternatively freeze, unbaked, up to 3 weeks in advance. Defrost overnight in refrigerator. Cook in preheated 200°C (400°F) Gas 6 oven for 30 minutes.
Make bechamel up to 2 days in advance. Cover with clingfilm, pressing down on the surface to prevent a skin forming. Refrigerate. Before using, beat to make it easy to spread. If making with cold bechamel, be sure to have ragù and pasta also cold.

**COOKS' NOTE**
We don't recommend no-cook lasagne, but if it is all you can find on the supermarket shelves, always treat it as regular dried lasagne and pre-cook until just pliable, about 30 seconds. Alternatively, follow the lasagne recipe on the packet, which will make proper allowances for the amount of liquid absorbed by the lasagne during baking.

**VARIATION**
# CLASSIC ITALIAN-AMERICAN LASAGNE
Omit bechamel. Use 250g (8oz) ricotta, crumbled, and 250g (8oz) finely sliced mozzarella in place of bechamel. Arrange in layers as directed, substituting ricotta and mozzarella mixture for bechamel. Bake as directed.

# PASTA WITH OLIVES AND OLIVE OIL

# OLIVE OIL IN THE PASTA PANTRY

Always use olive oil when cooking pasta sauces.

We buy extra virgin olive oil, which is made from the first pressing of the olives. It may cost a little more, but its superior quality makes it worth the extra expense. The relative cost of good extra virgin olive oil is not excessive when compared to a bottle of fine wine, which is finished at one sitting.

However, there is no need to use the best quality olive oil for everything. It is a good idea to have at least 2 bottles on the go at once. You can use a lighter, less costly oil for cooking and keep a superior one for seasoning and drizzling. Although both oils should be extra virgin, there's no need to buy anything but the least expensive available to use for cooking. Your choice of oil for drizzling and tossing is entirely personal. It shouldn't necessarily be Italian; we suggest that you try out a few, from different regions in Italy as well as from different countries, until you find one you like.

The colour of olive oil is dependent upon the timing of the harvest – the very dark green olive oil is from an early harvest, while later harvests yield golden oil – but this is not in itself an indication of quality. Unlike wine, olive oil does not improve with age. It is best stored in a cool, dark place at around 10°C-15°C (50°F-60°F) and should not be kept for longer than 1 year, as, after a year, many oils will start to taste stale.

Green and black olives are not interchangeable. Their taste and texture are different. Black olives owe their dark, rich flavour to being harvested when fully ripe. Green olives are picked before they are ripe and have a firm texture and a tangy taste. Olives are best bought loose and in small quantities as they will spoil within a few days unless generously covered with olive oil. Always have a few jars or tins of good quality olives on hand as a standby.

NO COOK
# OLIVE OIL

**SERVES 4**

**500g (1lb) dried pasta**
**8 tbs extra virgin olive oil**
**salt, crushed chilli flakes**

Cook pasta in a large pot of boiling, salted water, until firm to the bite. Drain, reserving ½ cup pasta water. Toss pasta with oil, adding reserved water as needed. Add salt and chilli flakes to taste.

**WHICH PASTA?**
Strands - spaghettini, spaghetti.

**COOKS' NOTE**
We like to use a rich, peppery Tuscan or Umbrian olive oil for this recipe, where the flavour of the olive oil is so important.

**VARIATIONS**

## LEMON OLIVE OIL

Add ½ tsp grated lemon zest and 2 tbsp lemon juice with the olive oil to pasta.

## GARLIC OLIVE OIL

Add 2 crushed garlic cloves with the olive oil to pasta.

## FRESH HERB OLIVE OIL

Add 1 handful of fresh flat-leaf parsley or basil, chopped, with the olive oil to pasta.

NO COOK
# CHILLI OLIVE PESTO

**SERVES 4**

125g (4oz) pitted black or
 green olives
1 garlic clove, crushed
½ tsp crushed chilli flakes
6 tbsp extra virgin olive oil
500g (1lb) dried pasta
salt, black pepper

Place olives, garlic, chilli flakes and oil
in a food processor or blender; pulse
until blended but still retaining some
texture. Cook pasta in a large pot of
boiling, salted water, until firm to the
bite if serving hot or just firm to the bite
if serving as a salad. Drain, reserving
½ cup pasta water. Return pasta with
pesto to the warm pasta pot. Toss well
to coat, adding reserved water as needed.
Add salt and pepper to taste. Serve
immediately or at room temperature.

**WHICH PASTA?**
Strands or thin ribbons - spaghetti, spaghettini,
linguine.

NO COOK
# OLIVE, ANCHOVY AND CAPER PESTO

**SERVES 4**

125g (4oz) pitted black olives
4 anchovy fillets, drained
2 tbsp drained capers, rinsed
1 garlic clove, crushed
¼ tsp dried thyme
6 tbsp olive oil
500g (1lb) dried pasta

Place olives, anchovies, capers, garlic,
thyme and oil in a food processor or
blender; pulse to a paste. Cook pasta in a
large pot of boiling, salted water, until
firm to the bite if serving hot or just firm
to the bite if serving as a salad. Drain,
reserving ½ cup pasta water. Return
pasta with pesto to the warm pasta
pot. Toss well to coat, adding reserved
water as needed. Serve immediately or
at room temperature.

**WHICH PASTA?**
Small shapes - pennette, conchiglie, fusilli.

**THINK AHEAD**
Make pestos up to 4 days in advance. Cover and
refrigerate. If serving as a salad, dress pasta up
to 8 hours in advance. Cover and store at room
temperature.

QUICK COOK
# SPICY LEMON OLIVE

**SERVES 4**

**500g (1lb) dried pasta**
**5 tbsp extra virgin olive oil**
**2 wide strips thinly pared lemon rind**
**1 - 50g (1¾ oz) tin anchovy fillets,**
**drained and chopped**
**15 pitted black olives, sliced**
**2 cloves garlic, finely chopped**
**½ tsp crushed chilli flakes**
**salt, black pepper**
**4 tbsp chopped fresh flat-leaf parsley**
**freshly grated pecorino romano**
**to serve**

Cook pasta in a large pot of boiling, salted water, until firm to the bite. While pasta is cooking, heat oil in a large frying pan. Add lemon rind and cook over low heat until sizzling, 2 minutes. Add anchovies and cook, stirring constantly, until disintegrated, 2-3 minutes. Add olives, garlic and chilli flakes. Cook until fragrant, 2 minutes. Add salt and pepper to taste. Remove and discard lemon rind. Drain pasta, reserving ½ cup pasta water. Add pasta with parsley to the hot sauce. Toss well to coat, adding reserved water as needed. Serve immediately with pecorino.

### WHICH PASTA?
Shapes or shells - fusilli, conchiglie, farfalle.

### COOKS' NOTE
Preserved anchovy fillets must be cooked over a gentle heat or they will become bitter. We recommend either Tuscan or Pugliese olive oil in this recipe.

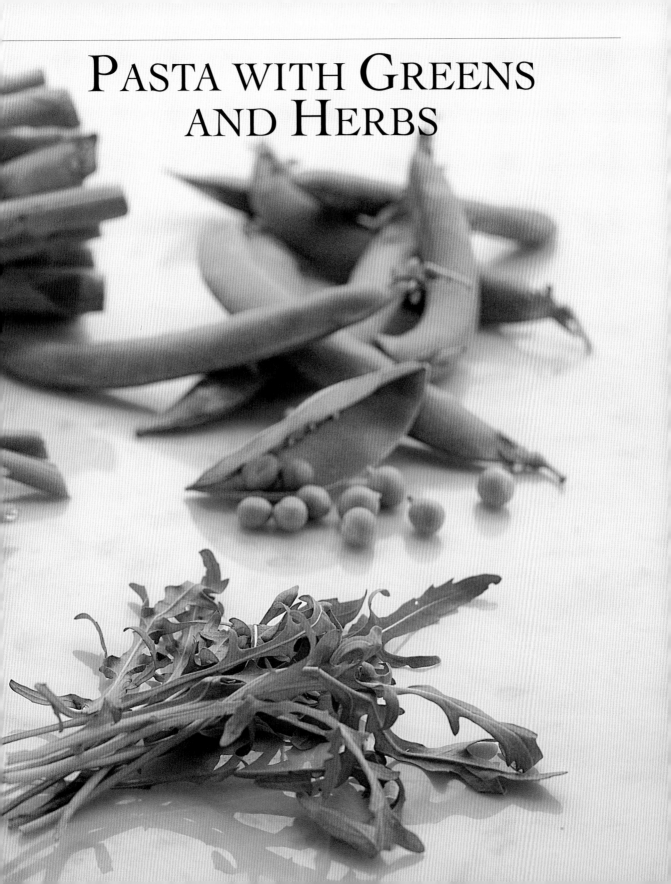

# PASTA WITH GREENS AND HERBS

# GREENS AND HERBS IN THE PASTA PANTRY

When buying fresh herbs, choose as you would fresh flowers. They should be vibrant green and bursting with life. The less fresh the herb, the less flavour it has. Fresh parsley and basil are the most essential fresh herbs in the pasta pantry, and dried just will not do as an alternative.

We prefer flat-leaf parsley, as it is more aromatic than the curly variety. Chopped parsley freezes well; store in an airtight container and scoop out a tablespoon or so as needed. Basil is best torn rather than chopped, as chopping damages its delicate flavour and colour.

Bunches of fresh herbs can be stored in the refrigerator, either in a glass of water with a plastic bag placed loosely over them, or in a plastic tub with their stalks removed. Choose greens that are firm, crisp and fresh looking. Cauliflower and broccoli should have juicy-looking stalks that show no signs of discolouring. Choose bright-looking courgettes that are very firm. When buying fresh peas, look for bright, snappy pods. Frozen peas are a perfectly acceptable substitute for fresh; in fact they are highly preferable to anything but locally grown new season peas in the pod.

NO COOK
# SIMPLE BASIL PESTO

**SERVES 4**

**60g (2oz) fresh basil leaves**
**2 garlic cloves**
**2 tbsp pine nuts**
**100ml (3½ floz) extra virgin olive oil**
**7 tbsp freshly grated parmesan**
**salt**
**500g (1lb) dried pasta**

Place basil, garlic, pine nuts and olive oil in a food processor; pulse until smooth. Transfer to a bowl. Stir in parmesan until well combined. Add salt to taste. Set aside or store, see below. Cook pasta in a large pot of boiling, salted water, until firm to the bite if serving hot or just firm to the bite if serving as a salad. Drain pasta, reserving ½ cup pasta water. Return pasta with the pesto to the warm pasta pot. Toss well to coat, adding reserved water as needed. Serve immediately or at room temperature.

**WHICH PASTA?**
Thin ribbons or strands - trenette, linguine, spaghetti, spaghettini.

**THINK AHEAD**
Make pesto up to 4 days in advance. Cover and refrigerate. Alternatively, make pesto without parmesan and freeze for up to 3 months. Add parmesan and seasoning when defrosted. If serving as a salad, dress pasta up to 8 hours in advance. Cover and store at room temperature.

**COOKS' NOTE**
Traditionally, pesto is made only with a sweet-flavoured olive oil, such as Ligurian.

**VARIATIONS**
## BEST BASIL PESTO
Make pesto as directed, adding 3 tbsp softened unsalted butter to the basil mixture with the parmesan.

## BASIL PESTO CREAM
Make pesto as directed, adding 3 tbsp Greek-style yoghurt or crème fraîche to the basil mixture with the parmesan.

NO COOK
# EVEN SIMPLER BASIL PESTO

**SERVES 4**

**500g (1lb) dried pasta**
**60g (2oz) fresh basil leaves, torn**
**2 tbsp pine nuts, toasted (see page 160)**
**2 garlic cloves, crushed**
**6 tbsp freshly grated parmesan**
**7 tbsp extra virgin olive oil**
**salt**

Cook pasta in a large pot of boiling, salted water, until just firm to taste. Drain, reserving ½ cup pasta water. Return pasta with basil, pine nuts, garlic, parmesan and oil to the warm pasta pot. Toss well to coat, adding reserved water as needed. Add salt to taste. Serve immediately.

**WHICH PASTA?**
Shapes or tubes - conchiglie, penne, ditali.

NO COOK
# SPINACH AND WALNUT PESTO

**SERVES 4**

**45g (1½ oz) stemmed spinach leaves**
**4 garlic cloves, crushed**
**3 tbsp walnut pieces**
**6 tbsp extra virgin olive oil**
**8 tbsp freshly grated parmesan**
**salt, black pepper**
**500g (1lb) dried pasta**

Place spinach, garlic, walnuts and oil in a food processor
or blender; pulse until smooth. Transfer to a bowl. Mix in
parmesan until well combined. Add salt and pepper to taste.
Set aside or store, see below.
Cook pasta in a large pot of boiling, salted water until firm
to the bite if serving hot or just firm to the bite if serving as a
salad. Drain, reserving ½ cup pasta water. Return pasta with
pesto to the warm pasta pot. Toss well to coat, adding reserved
water as needed. Serve immediately or at room temperature.

**WHICH PASTA?**
Large pasta tubes or shells - rigatoni, gnocchetti rigati, conchiglie.

**THINK AHEAD**
Make pesto up to 4 days in advance. Cover and refrigerate. Alternatively, make
pesto without cheese and freeze for up to 3 months. Add cheese and
seasoning when defrosted. If serving as a salad, dress pasta up to 8 hours in
advance. Cover and store at room temperature.

**VARIATION**
## PARSLEY PESTO
Replace spinach with 45g (1½ oz) fresh flat-leaf parsley. Make
as directed.

QUICK COOK
# FRAGRANT FRESH HERB

**SERVES 4**

**500g (1lb) dried pasta**
**8 tbsp extra virgin olive oil**
**1 garlic clove, finely**
**chopped**
**1 handful fresh flat-leaf**
**parsley, finely chopped**

**2 tbsp finely chopped**
**fresh oregano, marjoram**
**or basil**
**½ tbsp finely chopped fresh**
**rosemary, thyme or sage**
**salt, black pepper**

Cook pasta in a large pot of boiling, salted water, until firm to
the bite. While pasta is cooking, heat oil in a large frying pan.
Add garlic and herbs, and cook over medium heat until fragrant,
1 minute. Add salt and pepper to taste. Drain pasta, reserving
½ cup pasta water. Add pasta to the hot sauce. Toss well to
coat, adding reserved water as needed. Serve immediately.

**WHICH PASTA?**
Thin ribbons - linguine, spaghettini.

**COOKS' NOTE**
You can vary the kind of herbs, depending on what you have in the garden or
you find in the shop, but parsley must always be included.

## SIZZLING SAGE BUTTER

**SERVES 4**

**500g (1lb) dried pasta**
**90g (3oz) butter**
**2 garlic cloves, peeled and halved**
**16 fresh sage leaves**
**freshly grated parmesan to serve**

Cook pasta in a large pot of boiling, salted water, until firm to the bite. While pasta is cooking, heat butter and garlic in a small frying pan over a medium heat until just golden. Add sage leaves and cook, stirring, until fragrant, 30 seconds. Remove and discard garlic. Drain pasta and return to the warm pasta pot. Add hot butter and sage to pasta. Toss well to coat. Serve immediately with plenty of parmesan.

**WHICH PASTA?**
Medium ribbons or stuffed pasta - fettuccine, tagliatelle, ravioli, tortellini, cappelletti.

## FRESH HERBS AND GOLDEN CRUMBS

**SERVES 4**

**500g (1lb) dried pasta**
**5 tbsp extra virgin olive oil**
**75g (2½ oz) fresh breadcrumbs**
**4 spring onions, finely chopped**
**1 handful fresh flat-leaf parsley, basil, oregano or a combination**
**additional olive oil**
**salt, black pepper**

Cook pasta in a large pot of boiling, salted water, until firm to the bite. While pasta is cooking, heat oil in a large frying pan. Add breadcrumbs and cook, stirring constantly over medium-high heat, until crisp and golden, 5-8 minutes. Add spring onions and your choice of herbs and stir to combine. Drain pasta. Add drained pasta to the crumbs with 2 tbsp additional oil. Toss to coat. Add salt and pepper to taste. Serve immediately.

**WHICH PASTA?**
Strands or shapes - spaghetti, conchiglie, fusilli.

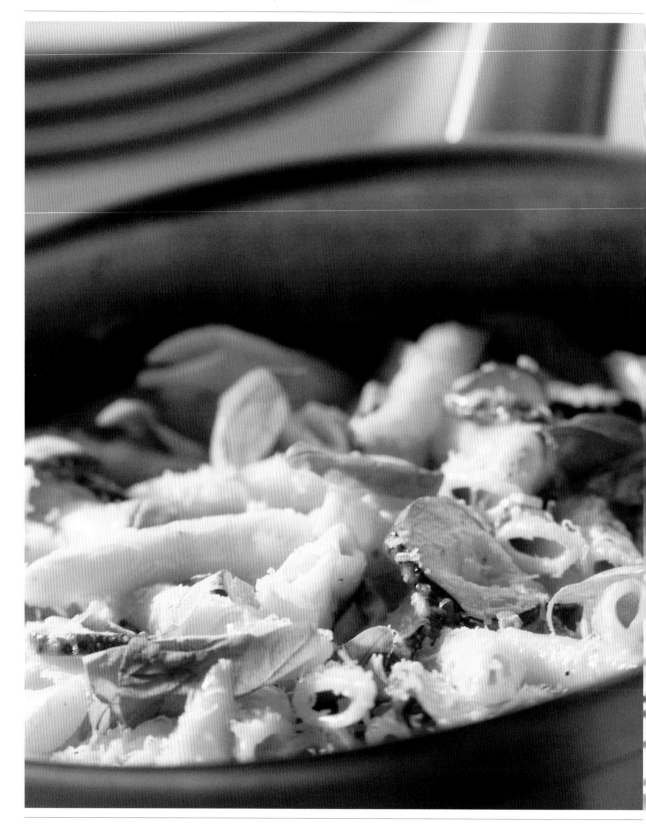

QUICK COOK
# COURGETTE AND BASIL WITH CREAM

**SERVES 4**

30g (1oz) butter
2 tbsp extra virgin olive oil
500g (1lb) small courgettes, cut
  into 0.5cm (¼ in) thick slices
4 garlic cloves, finely chopped
300ml (10floz) double cream
1 handful torn fresh basil leaves
salt, black pepper
500g (1lb) dried pasta
4 tbsp freshly grated parmesan,
  plus additional to serve

Melt butter with olive oil in a large frying pan. Add courgettes and cook, stirring frequently over medium-high heat, until just golden, 10 minutes. Reduce heat to medium-low. Add garlic and cook, stirring occasionally, until courgettes are soft, 5-10 minutes. Add cream and simmer gently until just thickened, 2 minutes. Add basil with salt and pepper to taste. Meanwhile, cook pasta in a large pot of boiling, salted water, until firm to the bite. Drain. Add pasta with parmesan to the hot sauce. Toss well to coat. Serve immediately with additional parmesan.

**WHICH PASTA?**
Tubes or shapes - farfalle, penne, ditali.

**VARIATION**
## COURGETTE WITH HAM
Add 4 ham slices cut into short, fine strips, 2.5cm (1in) long and 0.5cm (¼ in) wide, to the courgettes with the garlic. Finish as directed.

QUICK COOK
# PEAS, PROSCIUTTO AND FRESH HERBS

**SERVES 4**

500g (1lb) fresh peas (unshelled weight) or
  250g (8oz) tiny frozen peas, defrosted
500g (1lb) dried pasta
90g (3oz) butter
125g (4oz) prosciutto slices, cut into short, fine strips,
  about 2.5cm (1in) long and 0.5cm (¼ in) wide
salt, black pepper
6 tbsp freshly grated parmesan
2 tbsp finely chopped fresh mint, basil or flat-leaf parsley, optional
additional freshly grated parmesan to serve

If using fresh peas, cook in boiling, salted water until just tender, 5-8 minutes. Drain. Cook pasta in a large pot of boiling, salted water, until firm to the bite. While pasta is cooking, melt butter in a large frying pan. Add peas and prosciutto and cook, stirring constantly over medium heat, until hot through, 2 minutes. Add salt and pepper to taste. Drain pasta, reserving ½ cup pasta water. Add pasta with parmesan and your chosen herb, if using, to the hot sauce. Toss well to coat, adding reserved water as needed. Serve immediately with additional parmesan.

**WHICH PASTA?**
Medium to wide ribbons - fettuccine, tagliatelle, pappardelle.

**VARIATION**
## ASPARAGUS, PROSCIUTTO AND FRESH HERBS
Omit peas. Cook 250g (8oz) small asparagus tips in boiling salted water until just tender, 2-3 minutes. Finish as directed.

QUICK COOK
## SPICY BROCCOLI WITH GOLDEN GARLIC

**SERVES 4**

**500g (1lb) broccoli, stalks chopped
  and head separated into florets
7 tbsp extra virgin olive oil
4 garlic cloves, finely sliced
½ tsp crushed chilli flakes
salt, black pepper
500g (1lb) dried pasta**

Cook broccoli in a pan of boiling, salted water until just tender, 3-5 minutes. Heat oil in a large frying pan. Add garlic and cook over medium-high heat until just golden, 2 minutes. Add drained broccoli and chilli flakes and cook, stirring occasionally, for 5 minutes. Add salt and pepper to taste. Meanwhile, cook pasta in a large pot of boiling, salted water until firm to the bite. Drain. Add pasta to the hot sauce. Toss well to coat. Serve immediately.

**WHICH PASTA?**
Shapes - orecchiette, gnocchi, conchiglie.

**COOKS' NOTE**
We like to use a peppery olive oil from Puglia or Tuscany in this recipe to complement the spicy chilli flakes.

**VARIATIONS**
### SPICY BROCCOLI WITH GOLDEN GARLIC AND ANCHOVIES
Add 4 drained, chopped anchovies to the oil with the garlic. Finish as directed.

### SPICY CAULIFLOWER WITH GOLDEN GARLIC
Omit broccoli. Cook 500g (1lb) cauliflower florets in boiling, salted water until just tender, 5-7 minutes. Drain. Finish sauce as directed.

### SPICY SPROUTING BROCCOLI WITH GOLDEN GARLIC
Omit broccoli. Replace with 500g (1lb) coarsely chopped sprouting broccoli. Finish as directed.

QUICK COOK
## ASPARAGUS WITH CREAM

**SERVES 4**

**500g (1lb) asparagus, cut into 2.5cm (1in) pieces,
  using only tips and tender parts of stem
500g (1lb) dried pasta
75g (2½ oz) unsalted butter
2 tbsp finely chopped onion
150ml (5floz) double cream
nutmeg, salt, black pepper
2 tbsp freshly grated parmesan, plus additional to serve**

Cook asparagus in a pan of boiling, salted water until just tender, 3-5 minutes. Drain and plunge into cold water to cool completely. Drain and reserve. Cook pasta in a large pot of boiling, salted water, until firm to the bite. While pasta is cooking, melt butter in a large frying pan. Add onion and cook, stirring occasionally over medium heat, until soft, 5 minutes. Add asparagus and cream and simmer gently until the cream is just thickened, 1-2 minutes. Add nutmeg, salt and pepper to taste. Drain pasta, reserving ½ cup pasta water. Add drained pasta with parmesan to the hot sauce. Toss gently, being careful not to break up asparagus tips and adding reserved water as needed. Serve immediately with additional parmesan.

**WHICH PASTA?**
Medium tubes or ribbons - ditali, macaroni, fettuccine, tagliatelle.

QUICK COOK
# SHREDDED COURGETTES WITH GOLDEN GARLIC

SERVES 4

**500g (1lb) dried pasta
6 tbsp extra virgin olive oil
4-6 garlic cloves, finely sliced
4 medium courgettes, grated
salt, black pepper
8 tbsp freshly grated parmesan, plus additional to serve**

Cook pasta in a large pot of boiling, salted water, until firm to the bite. While pasta is cooking, heat oil in a large frying pan. Add garlic and cook over high heat until just golden, 2 minutes. Add courgettes and cook, stirring constantly, until soft, 5 minutes. Add salt and pepper to taste. Drain pasta, reserving ½ cup pasta water. Add drained pasta with parmesan to the hot courgettes. Toss well to coat, adding reserved water as needed. Serve immediately with additional parmesan.

**WHICH PASTA?**
Medium shapes or ribbons - gnocchi, conchiglie, orecchiette, linguine, fettuccine, tagliatelle.

**VARIATIONS**
## WILTED SPINACH WITH GOLDEN GARLIC
Omit courgettes. Use 500g (1lb) spinach, stemmed and roughly chopped. Cook garlic as directed. Add spinach and cook, stirring constantly, until soft, 2 minutes. Finish as directed.

## WILTED LEEKS WITH GOLDEN GARLIC
Omit courgettes. Use 3 medium leeks, halved lengthwise and finely sliced. Cook garlic as directed. Add leeks and cook, stirring constantly, until wilted, 5 minutes. Cover and cook, stirring occasionally, until soft, 10 minutes. Finish as directed.

# PRIMAVERA

**SERVES 4**

**60g (2oz) butter**
**2 tbsp extra virgin olive oil**
**1 tbsp finely chopped onion**
**1 small garlic clove, finely chopped**
**1 medium carrot, diced**
**1 medium celery stalk, diced**
**1 small courgette, diced**
**125g (4oz) green beans, cut into 1cm (½ in) pieces**
**125g (4oz) asparagus, tips cut into 2.5cm (1in) lengths**
  **and tender parts of stem cut into 1cm (½ in) pieces**
**125g (4oz) tiny frozen peas, defrosted, or 250g (8oz)**
  **(unshelled weight) fresh peas, shelled**
**175ml - 250ml (6floz - 8floz) chicken or vegetable stock**
**salt, black pepper**
**freshly grated parmesan to serve**

Melt butter with oil in a large frying pan over medium low heat. Add onion and cook, stirring constantly, until just soft, 3 minutes. Add garlic, carrot, celery, courgette, green beans, asparagus and peas and cook, stirring frequently, until almost tender, 10 minutes. Add stock just to cover and simmer gently until the liquid has almost evaporated and the vegetables are soft, 10 minutes. Add salt and pepper to taste. Meanwhile, cook pasta in a large pot of boiling, salted water, until firm to the bite. Drain. Add drained pasta to the hot sauce. Toss well to coat. Serve immediately with parmesan.

**WHICH PASTA?**
Strands, thin ribbons or shapes - spaghetti, linguine, farfalle, gnocchi, conchiglie.

**THINK AHEAD**
Make sauce up to 1 day in advance. Cool completely. Cover and refrigerate. Reheat slowly over low heat, stirring gently.

**VARIATIONS**
## PRIMAVERA WITH CREAM
Make sauce as directed using only 45g (1½oz) butter. Stir in 150ml (5floz) double cream to finished sauce. Simmer gently until just thickened, 2 minutes. Serve as directed.

## PRIMAVERA PESTO
Make sauce as directed. Add 4 tbsp simple basil pesto (see page 105) or storebought basil pesto, with the drained pasta, to the hot sauce. Serve as directed.

SLOW COOK
# SPINACH AND RICOTTA LASAGNE

SERVES 4

**12 sheets dried or fresh egg lasagne**
**1kg (2lb) spinach, washed**
**250g (8oz) ricotta, crumbled**
**30g (1oz) butter, melted**
**salt, black pepper, nutmeg**
**8 tbsp freshly grated parmesan**

FOR BECHAMEL

**75g (2½ oz) butter**
**4½ tbsp plain flour**
**750ml (1¼ pints) milk**
**salt, black pepper, nutmeg**

Preheat oven to 180°C (350°F) Gas 4.

Cook pasta, 3 sheets at a time, in a large pot of boiling, salted water for half the time recommended on the package, or until pasta is pliable but slightly hard at the centre, 4 minutes for dried pasta, 1 minute for fresh pasta. Drain and place sheets in a single layer on tea towels.

Place wet spinach in a dry pan. Cover pan and place over medium heat and cook until tender, stirring frequently, about 5 minutes. Drain and as soon as it is cool enough to handle, squeeze dry with your hands and coarsely chop. Combine spinach, ricotta and butter. Add salt, pepper and nutmeg to taste. Set aside.

For bechamel, melt butter over medium heat in a heavy saucepan. Whisk in flour and cook until foaming, about 1 minute. Remove from heat and pour in milk gradually, whisking constantly. Return to heat and cook, whisking constantly, until sauce thickens, about 2 minutes. Bring to the boil and remove from heat. Add salt, pepper and nutmeg to taste.

Pour a thin layer of the bechamel just to cover the bottom of a 30cm x 20cm x 7.5cm (12in x 8in x 3in) buttered oven-proof dish. Lay 3 pasta sheets on top. Place one quarter of the spinach-ricotta mixture in an even layer onto the pasta. Pour over one quarter of the bechamel and sprinkle a quarter of the parmesan on top. Starting with another layer of 3 pasta sheets, repeat layers. Repeat layers again to finish, ending with parmesan. Bake until golden and bubbling, 20-30 minutes. Leave to stand for 5 minutes before serving.

WHICH PASTA?
Egg lasagne, fresh where possible.

COOKS' NOTE
We don't recommend no-cook lasagne, but if it is all you can find on the supermarket shelves, treat it as regular dried lasagne for this recipe and pre-cook until just pliable, about 30 seconds.

THINK AHEAD
Assemble lasagne and leave to cool completely. Cover, unbaked, and refrigerate up to 1 day in advance. Alternatively freeze, unbaked, up to 3 weeks in advance. Defrost overnight in refrigerator. Cook in preheated 200°C (400°F) Gas 6 oven for 30 minutes.
Make bechamel up to 2 days in advance. Cover with clingfilm, pressing down on the surface to prevent a skin forming. Refrigerate. Before using, return to room temperature and beat to make it easy to spread.

OTHER VEGETARIAN LASAGNES
## SPINACH, GORGONZOLA AND PINE NUT LASAGNE

Have ready 200g (7oz) crumbled gorgonzola and 4 tbsp pine nuts. Assemble lasagne as directed, covering each layer of spinach-ricotta mixture with one quarter gorgonzola and 1 tbsp pine nuts before covering with bechamel and parmesan. Finish as directed.

## AUBERGINE, BASIL AND MOZZARELLA LASAGNE

Omit spinach. Have ready 750g (1½ lb) diced aubergine, 250g (8oz) grated mozzarella and 1 handful torn fresh basil. Spread aubergine pieces out in a roasting pan and drizzle over 3 tbsp extra virgin olive oil. Roast in a preheated 200°C (400°F) Gas 6 oven until soft, 20 minutes. Add salt and pepper to taste. Assemble lasagne as directed, covering each layer of pasta with one quarter ricotta, one quarter aubergine dice, one quarter grated mozzarella and one quarter torn basil before covering with bechamel and parmesan. Finish as directed.

## MUSHROOM, GARLIC AND PARSLEY LASAGNE

Omit spinach. Have ready 750g (1½ lb) sliced brown or wild mushrooms, 2 tbsp extra virgin olive oil, 3 finely chopped garlic cloves and 1 handful finely chopped fresh flat-leaf parsley. Heat oil in large frying pan. Add mushrooms and garlic and cook, stirring constantly, over medium-high heat until just coloured, 5 minutes. Add parsley and remove from heat. Add salt and pepper to taste. Assemble lasagne as directed, covering each layer of pasta with one quarter ricotta and one quarter mushroom mixture before covering with bechamel and parmesan. Finish as directed.

# PASTA WITH BEANS
# AND LENTILS

# BEANS AND LENTILS IN THE PASTA PANTRY

Although dried, all pulses should still have a fresh, unwrinkled look. Dried beans, chickpeas and lentils should be eaten within 12 months of being harvested, so renew your pantry supply yearly. If kept any longer they can become too dry and never cook properly until tender, however long you soak or boil them.

Chickpeas need soaking at least overnight and can take up to 4 hours to cook until tender. Luckily, tinned chickpeas are a perfectly good substitute for dried if well rinsed before using. If you can take the time, chickpeas are nicer skinned. Place cooked chickpeas in a bowl and cover with water. Gently rub the chickpeas between your fingers. The skins will slip off and float, while the chickpeas will sink. When you have finished, pour off the water and the skins together.

Lentils are an excellent pantry basic, as you don't have to soak them before cooking. For a truly Italian flavour, choose the small, brown Umbrian lentils which keep their shape when cooked. The very best are labelled Castelluccio; seek them out in good supermarkets and gourmet or Italian stores. Grey-green French puy lentils are a good substitute as they also hold their shape well when cooked.

Fresh green beans should be firm and crisp-looking. Look for green beans that are bright and snap readily when you bend them. Avoid any that are dull or limp. Buy fresh broad beans in the pod and choose smooth pods without wrinkled skins or blackened ends. The broad bean season is short, but small frozen beans are a good substitute. Unless very fresh and tender, broad beans are best skinned. Plunge into boiling water for 1 minute to loosen skins. Cool in cold water before draining and peeling.

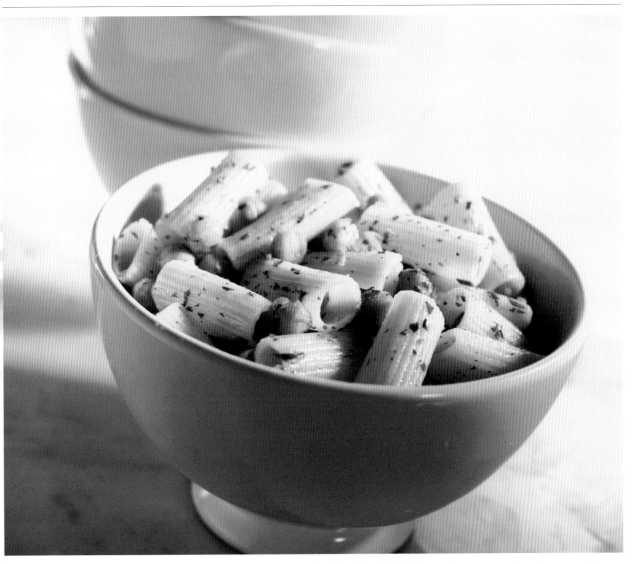

QUICK COOK
# CHICKPEAS WITH ROSEMARY, CHILLI AND GARLIC

**SERVES 4**

**500g (1lb) dried pasta**
**6 tbsp extra virgin olive oil**
**4 garlic cloves, finely chopped**
**½ tsp crushed chilli flakes**
**2 tsp finely chopped fresh rosemary or**
**  1 tsp dried rosemary, crumbled**
**1- 400g (14oz) tin chickpeas, drained and rinsed**
**2 tbsp finely chopped fresh flat-leaf parsley**
**additional extra virgin olive oil**
**salt, black pepper**

Cook pasta in a large pot of boiling, salted water, until firm to the bite. While pasta is cooking, heat oil in a large frying pan.

Add garlic, chilli flakes and rosemary and cook over medium-high heat until fragrant, 1 minute. Add chickpeas and cook until sizzling hot, 3 minutes. Drain pasta, reserving ½ cup pasta water. Add pasta with the parsley to the hot sauce. Toss well to coat, adding 2 tbsp additional olive oil, salt, pepper and reserved water as needed. Serve immediately.

**WHICH PASTA?**
Large tubes or shells - conchiglie, rigatoni, penne.

**VARIATION**
## BROAD BEANS WITH PECORINO
Cook just 2 garlic cloves with chilli flakes as directed. Omit rosemary and chickpeas. Replace with 500g (1lb) frozen broad beans, defrosted and cooked with 3 tbsp water until beans are tender and water has evaporated, 3-5 minutes. Add drained pasta with 4 tbsp freshly grated pecorino to hot sauce. Finish as directed.

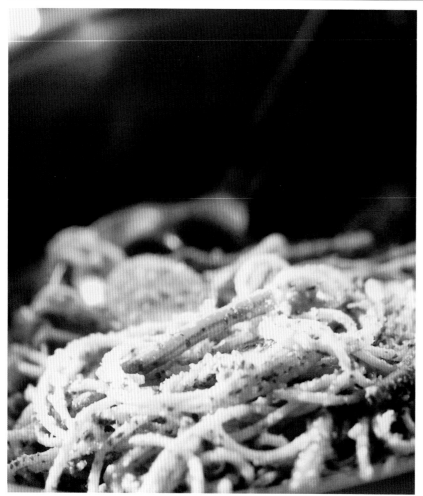

## BRAISED UMBRIAN LENTILS

SERVES 4 - 6

**300g (10oz) Umbrian or puy lentils**
**1 medium onion, cut in half**
**6 fresh sage leaves**
**2 fresh rosemary sprigs**
**1 tbsp salt**
**500g (1lb) dried pasta**
**4 fresh ripe tomatoes, peeled, seeded (see page 156) and chopped or**
**4 tinned Italian plum tomatoes, chopped**
**2 garlic cloves, finely chopped**
**1 handful fresh flat-leaf parsley, chopped**
**5 tbsp extra virgin olive oil, plus additional for serving**
**freshly grated pecorino or parmesan**

Place lentils, onion, sage, rosemary and salt in a large heavy-based pot. Cover with 3 litres (5 pints) cold water. Bring to a boil over a medium-high heat, stirring occasionally. Simmer gently until tender, 15-20 minutes. Bring water with lentils to a boil. Add pasta to pot and cook until pasta is just firm to the bite. Meanwhile, place tomatoes, garlic, parsley and oil in a large frying pan over medium-low heat. Cook until tomatoes soften, 3-4 minutes. When pasta is just firm to the bite, use a slotted spoon to transfer pasta and lentils to the pan, removing and discarding onion pieces and herbs. Turn heat to medium-high and cook, stirring constantly, 2-3 minutes. Serve immediately, with 5 tbsp additional olive oil and the grated cheese.

**WHICH PASTA?**
Shapes - conchiglie, gnocchi.

**COOKS' NOTE**
It is worth trying to find small, brown Umbrian lentils (see page 122). They give this dish an authentic flavour and texture.

## CLASSIC GENOESE PESTO

SERVES 4

**125g (4oz) fine green beans**
**4 small new potatoes, sliced 0.25cm (1/8 in) thick**
**500g (1lb) dried pasta**
**1 recipe simple basil pesto (see page 105)**
**3 tbsp extra virgin olive oil**
**salt**

Cook beans in a large pot of boiling salted water until tender, 5 minutes. Remove with a slotted spoon. Cool completely, by plunging into cold water, and reserve. Add potatoes to the pot and cook until tender in the centre when pierced with the tip of a small, sharp knife, 6-8 minutes. Remove with a slotted spoon and reserve. Add pasta to the pot and cook until firm to the bite if serving hot or just firm to the bite if serving as a salad. Return beans and potatoes to pot just before draining pasta, to heat through, 1 minute. Drain pasta, beans and potatoes, reserving 1/2 cup water. Return pasta, beans and potatoes with the pesto and olive oil to the warm pasta pot. Toss well, adding reserved water as needed. Add salt to taste. Serve immediately or at room temperature.

**WHICH PASTA?**
Strands or thin ribbons - linguine, trenette, spaghetti.

**THINK AHEAD**
Cook beans and potatoes up to 1 day in advance. Cool completely. Cover.
If serving as a salad, dress pasta up to 8 hours in advance. Cover and store at room temperature.

# PASTA WITH GARLIC

# GARLIC IN THE PASTA PANTRY

When choosing garlic, look for firm, plump bulbs. Cloves that are shrivelled will be dry with a musty, slightly metallic taste. Before chopping, we advise cutting garlic cloves in half and removing the inner green stem, as it has a slightly bitter flavour. New season fresh garlic is sweet and tender and can be used liberally.

For only a hint of garlic flavour, peel a clove of garlic, cut in half and cook in the butter or oil, removing and discarding when golden. Some cooks put a wooden toothpick through the garlic clove so it can be spotted easily and removed whenever it has released enough flavour.

When frying garlic, take care not to let it burn because it will give a bitter taste to the sauce.

Store garlic in a cool, dark place. The simplest way to peel garlic is to crush it with the flat side of a large knife (see page 156).

QUICK COOK
# OLIO AGLIO

**SERVES 4**

**500g (1lb) dried pasta**
**8 tbsp extra virgin olive oil**
**4 garlic cloves, finely chopped**
**salt, black pepper**

Cook pasta in a large pot of boiling, salted water, until firm to the bite. While pasta is cooking, heat oil in a large frying pan. Add garlic and cook, stirring occasionally over medium heat until golden, 2 minutes. Add salt and pepper to taste. Drain pasta. Add drained pasta to oil and garlic in the pan. Toss well to coat. Serve immediately.

**WHICH PASTA?**
Strands - spaghetti, spaghettini.

**VARIATIONS**

## OLIO AGLIO PEPERONCINO
Add ½ tsp crushed chilli flakes with garlic. Finish as directed.

## OLIVE OIL, GARLIC AND PARSLEY
Add 3 tbsp chopped fresh flat-leaf parsley with garlic. Finish as directed.

## OLIVE OIL, GARLIC AND FRESH TOMATO
Add 3 ripe fresh tomatoes, peeled, seeded (see page 156) and chopped with garlic. Finish as directed.

QUICK COOK
# ROAST GARLIC AND CHERRY TOMATOES

**SERVES 4**

**1kg (2lb) cherry tomatoes, halved**
**16 garlic cloves, peeled**
**8 tbsp extra virgin olive oil**
**¼ tsp crushed chilli flakes**
**½ tsp salt**
**¼ tsp black pepper**
**500g (1lb) dried pasta**
**1 handful torn fresh basil leaves**

Preheat oven to 200°C (400°F) Gas 6. Arrange tomatoes and garlic cloves so that they fit snugly in an oven tray or oven-proof pan. Drizzle with oil and sprinkle with chilli flakes, salt and pepper. Roast until garlic is soft and golden, 25 minutes.

Meanwhile, cook pasta in a large pot of boiling, salted water, until firm to the bite. Drain. Return pasta with tomatoes and garlic to the warm pasta pot. Toss well to coat. Sprinkle with basil. Serve immediately.

**WHICH PASTA?**
Strands - spaghettini, spaghetti.

**THINK AHEAD**
Roast tomatoes and garlic up to 1 day in advance. Cover and refrigerate. Reheat in preheated 200°C (400°F) Gas 6 oven for 10 minutes.

SLOW COOK
# GOLDEN GARLIC AND ONION

**SERVES 4**

60g (2oz) butter
3 tbsp extra virgin olive oil
8 garlic cloves, finely chopped
1lb (500g) onions, finely sliced
1 tsp sugar
salt
8 tbsp dry white wine
175ml (6floz) double cream
black pepper
500g (1lb) dried pasta
4 tbsp freshly grated parmesan,
    plus additional to serve

Melt butter and oil in a heavy-based pot over low heat. Add garlic, onion, sugar and 1 tsp salt. Cover and cook gently, stirring occasionally, until very soft, 30 minutes. Add 1 or 2 tbsp hot water to pan if necessary to prevent browning. Uncover and turn the heat to medium-high. Add wine and simmer until just evaporated, 2 minutes. Stir in the cream. Heat through and simmer until just thickened, 1-2 minutes. Add salt and pepper to taste. Meanwhile, cook pasta in a large pot of boiling, salted water, until firm to the bite. Drain and add pasta with parmesan to the hot sauce. Toss well to coat. Serve immediately with additional parmesan.

**WHICH PASTA?**
Strands or medium ribbons - spaghetti, paglia e fieno, fettuccine, tagliatelle.

**THINK AHEAD**
Make sauce up to 4 days in advance, omitting the cream. Cool sauce completely. Cover and refrigerate. Reheat and add cream just before serving. Finish as directed.

**COOK'S NOTE**
This is one of the traditional sauces from Emilia Romagna. Garlic is used very sparingly in this region. But we find that, being cooked for a long time, its flavour mellows and combines well with the onion.

**VARIATION**
# GOLDEN GARLIC, ONION AND FENNEL

Reduce the quantity of onions to 250g (8oz). Add 1 finely chopped large fennel bulb to the pan with the garlic, onions, sugar and salt. Cook and finish sauce as directed.

# Pasta with Peppers and Aubergines

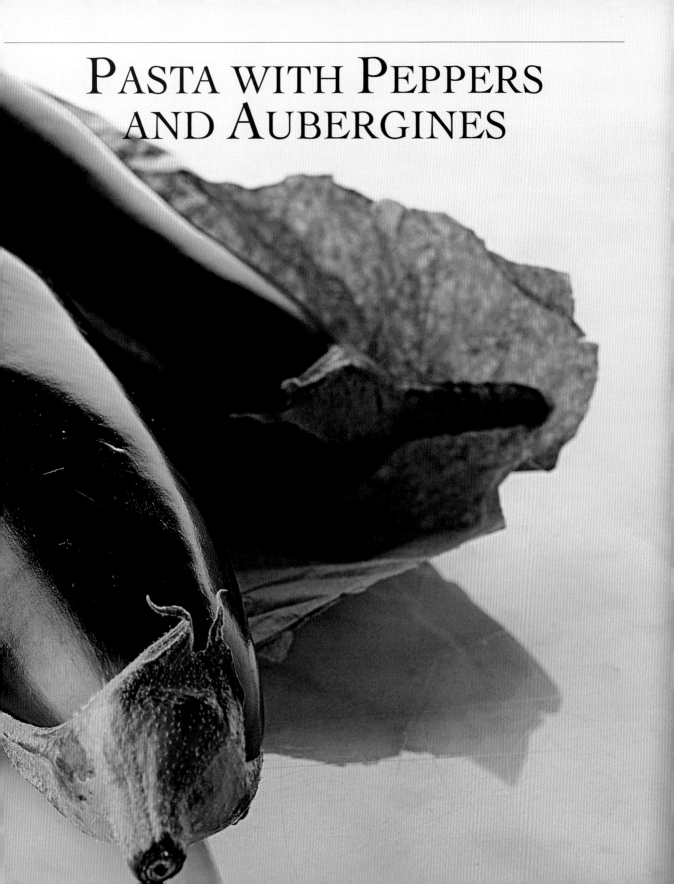

# PEPPERS AND AUBERGINES IN THE PASTA PANTRY

Choose aubergines with smooth, glossy and unblemished skins. There is no need to salt and de-gorge aubergines before using. The bitter juices that made this process essential in the past have been bred out of most modern aubergine varieties.

Peppers should be shiny, firm and crisp, with no wrinkles. Hold a pepper in your hand before buying. The heavier the pepper, the better it is, as it will have meatier and juicier flesh. Colour is an indication of ripeness, so, for optimum sweetness, choose the deepest red peppers.

Roasting and peeling peppers is well worth the extra effort. Roasting peppers brings out their flavour, while peeling removes the papery, indigestible skin.

Roast whole peppers under a hot grill, turning as needed until charred and wrinkled on all sides, 10-15 minutes. Wrap in a plastic bag or place in a bowl with a plate on top and leave until cool. The steam released by the peppers as they cool will loosen the skin.

To peel, remove pepper from bag or bowl. Peel off the charred skin, using the tip of a small knife. Scrape rather than rinse off any remaining bits of skin; rinsing washes away flavour. You can roast and peel peppers up to a week in advance. Cover with oil and refrigerate.

Although ready roast peppers in jars are a quick substitute for fresh roast peppers, they never really lose their distinctive "jar" taste.

# ROAST PEPPER

**SERVES 4**

**4 red peppers**
**6 tbsp extra virgin olive oil**
**2 garlic cloves, finely chopped**
**1/2 tsp crushed chilli flakes**
**salt, black pepper**
**500g (1lb) dried pasta**
**3 tbsp chopped fresh flat-leaf parsley**
**additional olive oil, optional**

Grill, peel and seed peppers (see page 157). Cut into strips 5cm (2in) long and 1cm (1/2 in) wide. Heat oil in a large frying pan. Add garlic and chilli flakes and cook over medium-high heat until fragrant, 1 minute. Add peppers and cook, stirring occasionally, until flavours are blended, 4 minutes. Add salt and pepper to taste. Meanwhile, cook pasta in a large pot of boiling, salted water, until firm to the bite. Drain. Add drained pasta with parsley to the hot peppers. Toss well. Drizzle with additional olive oil, if using. Serve immediately.

**WHICH PASTA?**
Large tubes - penne, rigatoni.

# AUBERGINE WITH CHILLI AND GARLIC

**SERVES 4**

**7 tbsp extra virgin olive oil**
**400g (14oz) aubergines, cut into 1cm ($\frac{1}{2}$ in) dice**
**4 garlic cloves, crushed**
**$\frac{1}{2}$ tsp crushed chilli flakes**
**2 tbsp tomato purée**
**1 tsp dried oregano**
**salt, black pepper**
**500g (1lb) dried pasta**
**additional olive oil to toss**

Heat oil in a large frying pan. Add aubergine, garlic and chilli flakes and cook, stirring frequently over high heat, until golden, 5-7 minutes. Turn down heat to medium-low. Stir in tomato purée and oregano and cook, stirring occasionally, until aubergine dice are soft and cooked through, 10 minutes. Add 2 tbsp hot water to the pan if the aubergine begins to stick. Add salt and pepper to taste. Meanwhile, cook pasta in a large pot of boiling, salted water, until firm to the bite. Drain. Add pasta with 2 tbsp additional olive oil to the hot sauce. Toss well to coat. Serve immediately.

**WHICH PASTA?**
Tubes or shapes - penne, rigatoni, orecchiette, conchiglie, fusilli.

**COOKS' NOTE**
To enhance the flavour of the spicy chilli flakes with the aubergine, we like to use a slightly peppery Tuscan or Pugliese olive oil.

**VARIATIONS**
## SICILIAN AUBERGINE WITH GARLIC
Add 2 tbsp capers and 10 sliced pitted black olives with the tomato purée and oregano. Finish as directed.

## AUBERGINE WITH MOLTEN MOZZARELLA
Make sauce as directed. Stir 250g (8oz) diced mozzarella into the finished sauce and heat gently until just melting, 1 minute. Add drained pasta to the hot sauce, omitting the additional olive oil. Finish as directed.

## SPICY AUBERGINE WITH GARLIC, BASIL AND PINE NUTS
Make sauce as directed. Add the drained pasta with 2 tbsp pine nuts and 1 handful torn fresh basil to the hot sauce.

## AUBERGINE WITH GARLIC AND RICOTTA
Make sauce as directed. Stir 125g (4oz) crumbled ricotta into the finished sauce and heat gently until warm through, 1 minute. Add drained pasta with 3 tbsp freshly grated pecorino to the hot sauce, omitting the additional olive oil.

## ROAST VEGETABLES WITH GREEN OLIVES AND RICOTTA

SERVES 4

1 aubergine, cut into 1cm
  (½ in) cubes
1 red or yellow pepper, cut into 1cm
  (½ in) pieces
1 small fennel bulb, cut into 1cm
  (½ in) pieces
4 ripe tomatoes, cut into quarters
6 whole garlic cloves, peeled
½ tsp crushed chilli flakes
5 tbsp extra virgin olive oil
salt, black pepper
500g (1lb) dried pasta
additional extra virgin olive oil
  for tossing
125g (4oz) pitted green olives
125g (4oz) ricotta, crumbled
1 handful fresh basil leaves
freshly grated parmesan to serve

Preheat oven to 200°C (400°F) Gas 6.
Toss aubergine, red or yellow pepper,
fennel, tomatoes and garlic with chilli
flakes and oil to coat well. Spread out
on a baking tray. Sprinkle with salt
and pepper. Roast until soft and lightly
charred, 20-25 minutes. Meanwhile,
cook pasta in a large pot of boiling,
salted water, until firm to the bite. Drain.
Return drained pasta to the warm pasta
pot and toss in 2 tbsp additional olive oil.
Add roasted vegetables to pasta and toss
well to coat. Add olives, ricotta and basil.
Serve immediately with parmesan.

**WHICH PASTA?**
Medium tubes - macaroni, pennette, ditali.

**THINK AHEAD**
Roast vegetables up to 1 day in advance.
Cover and refrigerate. Reheat in 200°C (400°F)
Gas 6 oven for 10 minutes before tossing with
cooked pasta.

## RED PEPPER PESTO

SERVES 4

2 large red peppers
2 garlic cloves
5 tbsp pine nuts, preferably toasted
  (see page 161)
¼ tsp crushed chilli flakes

½ tsp balsamic vinegar
5 tbsp extra virgin olive oil
salt, black pepper
500g (1lb) dried pasta
freshly grated parmesan to serve

Roast, peel and seed peppers (see page 157). Place peppers, garlic, pine nuts, chilli
flakes, vinegar and oil in a food processor; pulse until smooth. Add salt and pepper
to taste. Meanwhile, cook pasta in a large pot of boiling, salted water, until firm to
the bite. Drain, reserving ½ cup pasta water. Return drained pasta to the warm pasta
pot and add red pepper pesto. Toss well to coat, adding reserved water as needed.
Serve immediately with parmesan.

**WHICH PASTA?**
Strands or tubes - spaghetti, spaghettini, penne.

**THINK AHEAD**
Make pesto up to 3 days in advance. Cover and refrigerate.

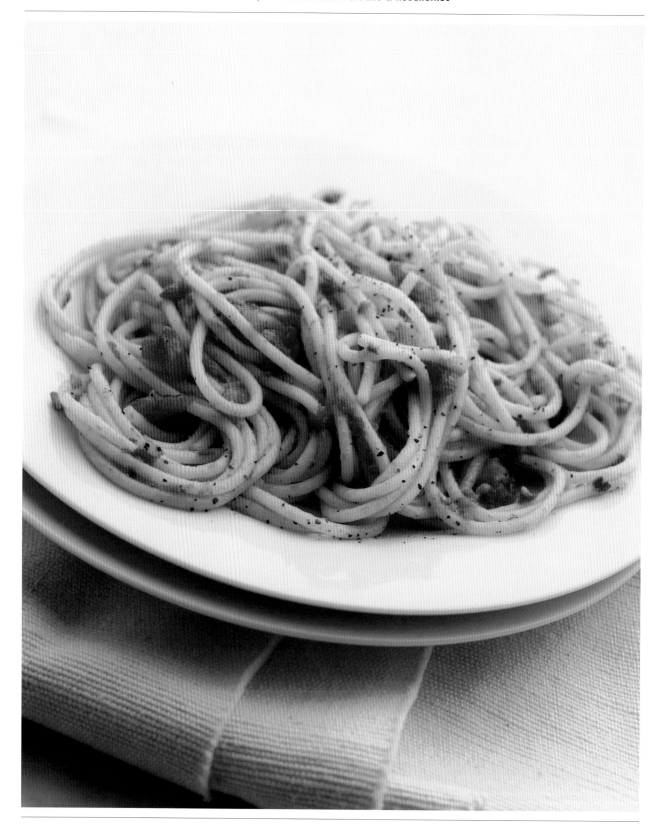

## SLOW COOK
# ROAST PEPPER AND TOMATO SAUCE

**SERVES 4**

**2 red peppers**
**6 tbsp extra virgin olive oil**
**1 garlic clove, crushed**
**$\frac{1}{4}$ tsp crushed chilli flakes**
**6 tomatoes, peeled, seeded**
  **(see page 156) and chopped**
**salt, black pepper**
**500g (1lb) dried pasta**

Roast, peel and seed peppers (see page 157) and finely chop. Heat oil in a large frying pan. Add garlic and chilli flakes and cook over medium heat until fragrant, 1 minute. Add tomatoes and cook, stirring occasionally, until thick, 20 minutes. Add peppers and cook to heat through and blend flavours, 5-10 minutes. Add salt and pepper to taste. Meanwhile, cook pasta in a large pot of boiling, salted water, until firm to the bite. Drain. Add drained pasta to the hot sauce. Toss well to coat. Serve immediately.

**WHICH PASTA?**
Strands or tubes - spaghetti, penne, ditali.

**THINK AHEAD**
Make sauce up to 3 days in advance. Cover and refrigerate.

**COOKS' NOTE**
A peppery Tuscan olive oil will enhance - and stand up to - the flavour of this lively, gutsy pasta sauce.

## SLOW COOK
# ROAST VEGETABLES AL FORNO

**SERVES 4**

**1 aubergine, cut into 1cm ($\frac{1}{2}$ in) dice**
**2 red peppers, cut into 1cm ($\frac{1}{2}$ in)**
  **dice**
**2 garlic cloves, crushed**
**$\frac{1}{4}$ tsp crushed chilli flakes**
**3 tbsp extra virgin olive oil**
**salt, black pepper**
**500g (1lb) dried pasta**
**1 recipe simmered tomato**
  **sauce (see page 42)**
**125g (4oz) ricotta, crumbled**
**125g (4oz) mozzarella, sliced**
**6 tbsp freshly grated parmesan**

Preheat oven to 200°C (400°F) Gas 6. Toss the aubergine and pepper pieces with garlic, chilli flakes and oil to coat well. Spread out evenly on a baking tray. Sprinkle with salt and pepper.

Roast until soft and lightly charred, 20-25 minutes. Meanwhile, cook pasta in a large pot of boiling, salted water, until just firm to the bite. Drain pasta and combine with with tomato sauce and roasted vegetables. Toss well to coat. Add salt and pepper to taste. Place half tossed pasta in an oiled 20cm x 20cm x 5cm (8in x 8in x 2in) oven-proof dish. Cover with ricotta, mozzarella and half the parmesan. Top with remaining pasta. Sprinkle with remaining parmesan. Bake until golden and bubbling, 10 minutes. Leave to stand for 5 minutes before serving.

**WHICH PASTA?**
Large tubes or shells - rigatoni, penne, conchiglie.

**THINK AHEAD**
Assemble, cover unbaked and refrigerate up to 8 hours in advance. Alternatively, cover unbaked and freeze up to 3 weeks in advance. Defrost overnight in refrigerator. Cook in preheated 200°C (400°F) Gas 6 oven for 30 minutes.

# FRESH & FILLED PASTA

# FRESH EGG PASTA

**SERVES 4**

**300g (10oz) italian 00 (doppio zero)
  or plain flour**
**½ tsp salt**
**3 eggs**
**additional flour for dusting**

ESSENTIAL EQUIPMENT
*pasta machine*

Mix the flour and salt into a bowl. Make
a well in the centre of the flour. Add eggs
to the well. With a fork, beat the eggs
and gradually draw in the flour. With
your hands, mix in as much of the flour
as needed to make a rough dough. You
may not need to incorporate all of the
flour. Or if the dough is too sticky, you
may need to sprinkle over a little
extra flour.

As soon as the dough begins to form a
ball, turn it out onto a work surface
lightly dusted with flour.

Knead the dough by pushing it away
from you with the heel of your hand.
Knead until smooth, elastic and no
longer sticky, 10 minutes. Wrap in
clingfilm and leave to rest for at least
30 minutes or up to 4 hours.

**COOKS' NOTE**
The finest fresh pasta is always made at home.
Homemade fresh pasta is simple, fun and very
satisfying to make. We advise making fresh pasta
by hand rather than in a food processor. Eggs vary
in size and different flours will absorb different
quantities of liquid on different days, depending
on whether you are working in a dry or humid
atmosphere. It's always easier to add more flour
to a dough that is too soft than correct a dough
that is too stiff. Working by hand allows you to
adjust the quantity of flour as you go along.

## ROLLING OUT FRESH PASTA

Set the pasta machine rollers on their widest setting. Cut the dough into 4 equal-sized pieces. Lightly dust 1 piece of dough with flour and flatten with your hand. Keep the remaining pieces wrapped in clingfilm. Feed 1 piece pasta dough through the rollers. Place the rolled strip flat on the table and fold in half. Feed the folded dough through the rollers again. Give the dough a quarter turn before feeding it each time through the machine, to ensure that it is evenly kneaded. Repeat folding and rolling out 5 or 6 times until the dough is smooth and silky. Reset the rollers to the next setting and feed the dough through the settings until you achieve the desired thickness (see below for tagliatelle, tagliolini or lasagne; see page 146 for ravioli). If the dough sticks to the machine, dust both sides lightly with flour.

### THINK AHEAD

Make, roll and cut dough up to 5 days in advance. Leave to dry out, then store at room temperature in single layers on paper towels set over a tray. Cover with a clean tea towel. Alternatively, freeze for up to 4 months. Leave to dry out, then place in freezer bags or an airtight container. Freeze.

### FRESH TAGLIATELLE OR TAGLIOLINI

Roll the dough through the machine on the second to thinnest setting. Lay each pasta sheet on a clean tea towel, letting about one third of its length hang down over the edge of the work surface. Leave until the pasta is dry to the touch but still pliable, about 10-30 minutes. Feed each sheet of dough through the broad cutters of the machine for tagliatelle or through the narrow ones for tagliolini. As the strips emerge, catch them on your hand. Sprinkle with a little semolina or plain flour, then coil loosely into a bundle. Place on a clean tea towel and repeat with remaining dough. The pasta strands are now ready to be cooked. Alternatively, place in a single layer on clean tea towels until dry, about 24 hours.

### FRESH LASAGNE

Roll out the dough on the last setting of the machine. Cut each pasta sheet into squares about 12 x 8.5cm (5 x 3½in). Cook immediately or leave to ry as for tagliatelle or tagliolini.

# FRESH RAVIOLI

**SERVES 4**
**1 recipe pasta dough (see page 144)**
**1 recipe pasta filling (see page 147)**
**plain flour or semolina for dusting**
ESSENTIAL EQUIPMENT
*pasta machine, pastry brush, fluted*
*pastry wheel*

Roll the dough through the machine on
the second to thinnest setting (see page
145). Cut the dough sheets into 50cm
(20in) lengths. Cover the dough sheets
with clingfilm to keep them pliable until
you are ready to shape them.

Fold the sheet in half to make a crease
down the centre. Unfold. Using the
crease as a guide, place teaspoonfuls
of the filling at 4cm (1½ in) intervals in
2 rows along opposite sides of the crease.
Lightly brush the pasta around the filling
with water. Lay over a second pasta
sheet to cover the filling. With your
fingertips, press gently around each
mound of filling to seal the dough and
to push out any pockets of air. Cut into
squares with a fluted pastry wheel.

Place the squares upside down on a
clean tea towel, making sure they do not
touch. Repeat with remaining dough.
The ravioli are now ready to be cooked.
Alternatively, leave to dry on clean tea
towels, turning over occasionally, until
the dough has dried out completely,
about 24 hours.

Cook the ravioli in gently boiling,
salted water under tender to the bite,
4-7 minutes. To drain, scoop out with a
slotted spoon and shake off excess water.
Place in a warmed bowl and toss gently
to coat with sauce. Serve immediately.

**THINK AHEAD**
Make ravioli up to 3 days in advance. Leave to dry
out, then store on layers of greaseproof paper in an
airtight container in the refrigerator. Alternatively,
freeze for up to 2 months. Spread ravioli in a single
layer on a baking sheet, making sure that the edges
are not touching. Place in freezer uncovered until
hard, 30 minutes. Once the ravioli are frozen, pack
into zip-lock bags or an airtight container and
return to the freezer. Frozen ravioli should be
cooked from frozen, allowing an extra 5 minutes
of cooking time.

## GREENS, PARMESAN AND RICOTTA FILLING

**SERVES 4**

**1kg (2lb) spinach or swiss chard,
  washed and stemmed
250g (8oz) ricotta
8 tbsp freshly grated parmesan
salt, pepper, nutmeg
2 eggs**

Wash but do not dry spinach. Place wet spinach in a covered pan over a medium heat. Cook, stirring occasionally, until tender, 5 minutes. Drain and leave to cool. Squeeze out excess water with your hands. Chop finely and combine with ricotta and parmesan. Add salt, pepper and nutmeg to taste. Add eggs and mix to a stiff paste.

**WHICH SAUCE?**
Sizzling Sage Butter (see page 108), Butter and Parmesan (see page 47), Fresh Tomato (see page 37).

**VARIATIONS**

## RICOTTA AND HERB FILLING

Replace spinach with 2 handfuls chopped fresh basil or parsley. Combine basil or parsley with ricotta and parmesan. Finish as directed.

## PORCINI MUSHROOM FILLING

**SERVES 4**

**25g (1oz) dried porcini mushrooms
3 tbsp olive oil
2 garlic cloves, finely chopped
1 shallot, finely chopped
625g (20oz) brown or field
  mushrooms, finely chopped
2 tbsp finely chopped fresh
  flat-leaf parsley**

Soak porcini (see page 156) and finely chop. Heat oil in a large frying pan. Add garlic and shallots and cook over medium-high heat until fragrant, 1 minute. Add mushrooms and porcini and cook, stirring frequently, until crisp, 10 minutes. Add parsley and salt and pepper to taste. Leave to cool completely before using to fill ravioli.

**WHICH SAUCE?**
Fresh Tomato (see page 37), Butter and Parmesan (see page 47), All'Alfredo (see page 53).

**THINK AHEAD**
Make fillings up to 1 day in advance. Cover and refrigerate.

# THINK AHEAD TIPS

### COOKING PASTA FOR A BAKED DISH

When cooking pasta for a dish that will require further cooking, such as baked or layered pasta, the cooking time should be cut by approximately a third. Depending on the kind of pasta you are cooking, this means you should begin checking for doneness (see page 23) a couple of minutes early. Remove and drain the pasta when it is still slightly hard at the centre.

### PREPARING AN UNBAKED PASTA DISH FOR THE FREEZER

When preparing baked pasta dishes, such as lasagne, ahead of time, you will get better results if you prepare the dish and freeze it before baking.

If you wish to use the casserole dish while the assembled dish is stored in the freezer, line the casserole dish with heavy-duty aluminium foil, allowing enough foil to come over the sides of the dish to cover and seal the food.

Assemble the dish. Be sure that all the ingredients in the assembled dish are at room temperature before placing it in the freezer.

Do not cover the top with the extended foil at the sides. Freeze until solid, then use the sides to lift the frozen dish out of the casserole. Cover the frozen dish with the foil sides to seal. Place in a large zip-lock freezer bag and return to the freezer until ready to use.

### DEFROSTING AN UNBAKED PASTA DISH

Remove from freezer bag and place the frozen dish in the casserole in which it will be baked. Place in the refrigerator and allow the dish to thaw overnight, before baking.

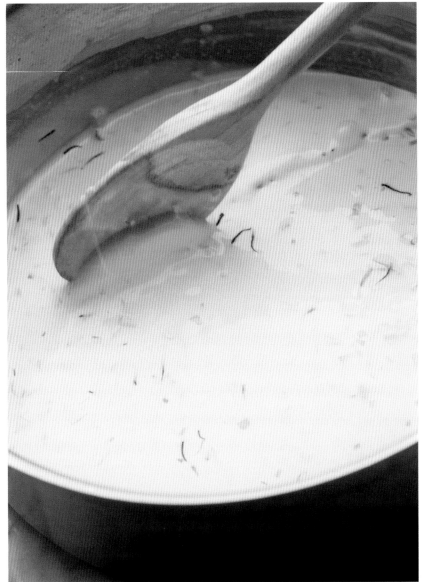

## DEFROSTING AND REHEATING PASTA SAUCES

Allow frozen pasta sauces to thaw overnight in the refrigerator.

When reheating a sauce, especially in the case of one that has been previously frozen, additional liquid will in most cases be needed to return the sauce to the proper consistency.

In the case of rich cream-based or meat sauces, use a few tablespoons of warm milk to add moisture and to retain the rich flavour. In the case of olive oil and tomato based sauces, remember to reserve about half a cup of the pasta water before draining the pasta. Use this, or part of it, to add both moisture and flavour back to the reheated sauce.

## MAKING AND FREEZING PASTA SAUCES

Be sure that the sauce has cooled completely before storing it in the freezer.

Choose a container for freezing that has a capacity as close to the actual volume of the sauce prepared as possible. The more oxygen permitted to surround frozen food, the greater the chance of freezer burn and spoilage.

The best way to freeze anything is in a zip-lock freezer bag. Transfer the cooled sauce to a zip-lock freezer bag, expelling as much air as possible before sealing it. Place on a plate until frozen solid then remove the plate.

# PASTA IN THE PANTRY

Fast food doesn't have to mean take-away when you have pasta in the pantry. Perfect for impromptu entertaining, pasta is the original convenience food. A well-stocked pantry is the key. With a few well-chosen staples (see below) in the kitchen cupboard, refrigerator or freezer, a simple meal can be on the table in the time it takes to boil water.

To save you scanning the index, we've compiled an easy reference **PASTA PLANNER** (see pages 152-153) that cross-refers ingredients with cooking time. You can select recipes at a glance, simply by matching your schedule to the contents of your shopping basket or pantry.

Pasta is unquestionably the most versatile of foods. It is an everyday food and a food for celebrations. It makes a last-minute supper for one and a satisfying meal for all the family. Refer to **PASTA ON THE MENU** (see pages 154-155) and you'll see that, whatever the season, the occasion, the time available or the cook's mood, pasta will serve.

## IN THE REFRIGERATOR

### PARMESAN
Buy in a piece and store in the warmest section of the refrigerator.

### BUTTER
Must be unsalted for pasta sauces.

### EGGS
Buy large and choose organic when possible.

### CREAM
For cooking, choose double cream or crème fraîche. Crème fraîche is a great pantry basic as it keeps longer than regular cream.

### LEMONS
Buy organic lemons when possible, but especially when the recipe calls for grated lemon zest, as organic lemons are not waxed or sprayed with chemicals.

## IN THE FREEZER

### UNSMOKED PANCETTA
Cut and wrap in 60g (2oz) pieces. Unsmoked streaky bacon is an acceptable alternative.

### FROZEN PEAS
Choose tiny, young *petits pois* when possible.

### PARSLEY
Buy a bunch of flat-leaf parsley, chop and keep in an airtight container for using as needed.

# IN THE CUPBOARD

## DRIED PASTA
Have a selection of shapes and a variety of sizes on hand.

## ANCHOVIES
Buy in tins or jars. Alternatively, have a tube of anchovy paste in the refrigerator (see page 160).

## TUNA
Choose tins of tuna packed in olive oil for best texture and taste. We prefer yellowfin and bonito to skipjack.

## TOMATOES
Choose tins of Italian brands for tastier, juicier tomatoes.

## CAPERS
Buy in jars, in brine or salt (see page 160).

## OLIVES
Black are the most useful in the pasta pantry.

## CRUSHED CHILLI FLAKES
Renew your supply yearly as dried chilli loses its kick over time.

## DRIED PORCINI
Buy packets with large pieces, which are from the mushroom caps. The smaller, crumblier pieces come from the stalks and have less flavour.

## ONIONS
Small yellow onions are the most useful.

## WHITE WINE
Choose a dry, light white wine.

## GARLIC
Choose milder pink-skinned garlic when possible.

## OLIVE OIL
Always buy extra virgin. We like to have a regular brand on hand for cooking, plus a bottle of premium oil for seasoning and drizzling.

## COARSE SALT
Sea salt is the choice of all food lovers because of its fuller flavour.

## BLACK PEPPERCORNS
Always buy whole peppercorns and freshly grind to order.

# PASTA PLANNER

| | MAKE AHEAD | NO COOK | QUICK COOK | SLOW COOK | AL FORNO |
|---|---|---|---|---|---|
| **ASPARAGUS** | | | • Asparagus with Cream<br>• Asparagus, Prosciutto & Fresh Herbs | | |
| **AUBERGINE** | | | • Aubergine with Chilli & Garlic | • Roast Vegetables with Green Olives & Ricotta | • RoastVegetables al Forno |
| **BASIL** | • Simple Basil Pesto | • Simple Basil Pesto<br>• Even Simpler Basil Pesto<br>• Lemon, Basil & Mascarpone | • Classic Genoese Pesto | | |
| **BEEF** | • Classic Ragù Bolognese<br>• Lasagne Al Forno | | • Pizzaiola | • Classic Ragù Bolognese | • Lasagne al Forno |
| **BROCCOLI** | | | • Spicy Broccoli | | |
| **BUTTER** | | • Butter & Parmesan | | | |
| **CHICKEN** | • Chicken, Tomato & Rosemary Ragù | | • Pan-Roast Chicken with Lemon & Mushrooms | • Chicken, Tomato & Rosemary Ragù | |
| **CREAM** | | • Cream & Parmesan | • Golden Saffron<br>• All'Alfredo | | |
| **GARLIC** | | | • Olio Aglio<br>• Roast Garlic & Cherry Tomatoes | • Golden Garlic & Onion | |
| **GORGONZOLA** | • 4 cheese | • Gorgonzola & Ricotta | • Gorgonzola Cream | | • 4 Cheese |
| **MOZZARELLA** | • 4 Cheese<br>• Tomato and Mozzarella al Forno | • 3 Cheese<br>• Fresh Tomato with Mozzarella | • Fresh Tomato Sauce with Molten Mozzarella<br>• Pan-Cooked Tomato & Mozzarella | • Tomato & Mozzarella Al Forno | • Tomato and Mozzarella al Forno |
| **MUSHROOMS** | • Mushroom al Forno | | • Wild Mushroom Persillade<br>• Mushroom, White Wine & Cream | | • Mushroom al Forno |
| **DRIED PORCINI** | • Tomato with Porcini | | • Porcini, White Wine & Cream | | • Mushroom al Forno |
| **OLIVES** | • Chilli Olive Pesto<br>• Olive, Anchovy & Caper Pesto | • Chilli Olive Pesto<br>• Olive, Anchovy & Caper Pesto | • Spicy Lemon Olive<br>• Puttanesca | | |
| **PANCETTA** | | | • Carbonara<br>• Crispy Pancetta with Spring Onions<br>• Amatriciana | | |

| | MAKE AHEAD | NO COOK | QUICK COOK | SLOW COOK | AL FORNO |
|---|---|---|---|---|---|
| **PARSLEY** | • Parsley Pesto | • Parsley Pesto<br>• Butter, Parmesan & Parsley | • Fresh Fragrant Herbs | | |
| **PEAS** | • Primavera | | • Peas, Prosciutto & Fresh Herbs<br>• Primavera<br>• Butter, Parmesan & Peas | | |
| **PEPPERS** | • Roast Vegetables al Forno<br>• Red Pepper Pesto<br>• Roast Pepper & Tomato Sauce | | • Roast Vegetables with Green Olives & Ricotta<br>• Red Pepper Pesto | • Roast Pepper & Tomato Sauce | • Roast Vegetables al Forno |
| **PRAWNS** | • Prawns with Lemon & Basil | • Prawns with Lemon & Basil | • Spicy Garlic Prawns with Cherry Tomatoes<br>• Chilli Prawns | | |
| **PROSCIUTTO** | | | • Prosciutto & Cream<br>• Peas, Prosciutto & Fresh Herbs | | |
| **SAUSAGE** | • Spicy Sausage Ragù | | • Sausage with Cream & Basil | • Spicy Sausage Ragù | |
| **SPINACH** | • Spinach & Walnut Pesto<br>• Spinach & Ricotta Lasagne | • Spinach & Walnut Pesto | • Wilted Spinach with Golden Garlic | • Spinach & Ricotta Lasagne | • Spinach & Ricotta Lasagne |
| **SMOKED SALMON** | | • Smoked Salmon, Vodka & Dill | • Smoked Salmon with White Wine, Cream & Chives | | |
| **TOMATOES**<br>**Fresh** | • Puttanesca<br>• Arrabbiata<br>• Napolitana<br>• Roast Tomato | | • Fresh Tomato<br>• Puttanesca<br>• Arrabbiata<br>• Napolitana | • Roast Tomato | |
| **Sun-dried** | • Red Pesto<br>• Sun-dried Tomato with Chilli, Garlic and Black Olives | • Red Pesto | | | |
| **Tinned** | • Puttanesca<br>• Arrabbiata<br>• Napolitana<br>• Tomato & Mozzarella al Forno<br>• Simmered Tomato | | • Puttanesca<br>• Arrabbiata<br>• Napolitana<br>• Pan-Cooked Tomato & Mozzarella | • Tomato & Mozzarella al Forno<br>• Simmered Tomato | • Tomato & Mozzarella al Forno |
| **TUNA** | • Tuna with Lemon & Capers<br>• Tuna & Tomato | • Tuna with Lemom & Capers | • Tuna & Tomato | | |

# PASTA ON THE MENU

## SHORT ORDER PASTA

*In a rush? Try these fast and simple sauces, based on a few fresh ingredients, that are on the table in less than 20 minutes.*

Butter, Parmesan & Asparagus
**(See page 47)**
Scallops with Garlic &
Crisp Crumbs
**(See page 68)**
Chicken with Lemon &
Mushrooms
**(See page 87)**
Lemon, Basil & Mascarpone
**(See page 51)**
Fresh Tomato Sauce with
Molten Mozzarella
**(See page 37)**
Smoked Salmon with
Vodka & Dill
**(See page 64)**
Pizzaiola
**(See page 83)**

## PASTA TO CELEBRATE SPRING

*Winter is finally over and the season's first fresh roots and shoots appear on the market. Why not celebrate, Italian-style?*

Peas, Prosciutto & Fresh Herbs
**(See page 111)**
Primavera
**(See page 116)**
Broad Beans with Pecorino
**(See page 123)**
Parsley Pesto
**(See page 107)**
Asparagus with Cream
**(See page 112)**

## PASTA SOLO

*There's no need to go without because it's just you at home this evening. Treat yourself! Pasta makes cooking for one fun.*

Olio Aglio
**(See page 129)**
Even Simpler Basil Pesto
**(See page 105)**
Three Cheese
**(See page 49)**
Salmon Caviar with
Butter & Chives
**(See page 66)**
Butter & Parmesan
**(See page 47)**
Fresh Herbs &
Golden Crumbs
**(See page 108)**

## SELF-SERVE PASTA FOR A BUFFET OUTDOORS

*Light, fresh and mayo-free, our pasta salads are more truly Italian than patio cuisine. Try one out and see, but we're confident you'll be converted!*

Fresh Tomato, Rocket &
Balsamic Vinegar
**(See page 33)**
Tuna with Lemon & Capers
**(See page 64)**
Classic Genoese Pesto
**(See page 124)**
Sun-Dried Tomato with Chilli,
Garlic & Black Olives
**(See page 33)**

## PASTA FOR CHILDREN

*Even babies in highchairs love pasta. Try these dishes out on young mouths: they'll soon be firm favourites with all the family.*

Simmered Tomato
**(See page 42)**
Butter, Parmesan & Peas
**(See page 47)**
Four Cheese Al Forno
**(See page 52)**
Tuna and Tomato
**(See page 69)**
Classic Ragù Bolognese
**(See page 91)**
Napolitana
**(See page 35)**

## DO-AHEAD DINNER PARTY PASTA

*Many pasta sauces can be prepared well in advance. Any of these simple recipes will make an elegant opener for six or a non-meat main for four. Refer to our Think Ahead notes.*

Spinach & Walnut Pesto
**(See page 107)**
Simmered Tomato
with Vodka
**(See page 42)**
Primavera with Cream
**(See page 116)**
Roast Vegetables with
Green Olives & Ricotta
**(See page 138)**
Roast Tomato with Pesto
**(See page 40)**

## COLD WEATHER COMFORT PASTA

*When the sky's grey and the wind bites, nothing beats a steaming bowl of pasta for lighting up faces around the table.*

Spicy Sausage Ragù
**(See page 91)**
Golden Garlic & Onion
**(See page 131)**
Braised Umbrian Lentils
**(See page 124)**
Ragù Al Forno
**(See page 92)**
Pan-Cooked Tomato & Mozzarella
**(See page 39)**

## IMPROMPTU PASTA

*With our well-chosen staples on hand (refer to Pasta in the Pantry on page 150) even the busiest of cooks can create a quick-fix meal in a matter of minutes.*

Tuna & Tomato
**(See page 69)**
All'Alfredo
**(See page 53)**
Olio Aglio Peperoncino
**(See page 129)**
Tomatoes with Porcini
**(See page 60)**
Butter, Parmesan & Peas
**(See page 47)**
Spicy Lemon Olive
**(See page 101)**

## PASTA ITALIA

*Simple, honest, traditional dishes full of the charm and flavour of Italy.*

Napolitana
**(See page 35)**
Carbonara
**(See page 88)**
Arrabbiata
**(See page 35)**
Puttanesca
**(See page 34)**
Olio Aglio Peperoncino
**(See page 129)**
Amatriciana
**(See page 87)**

## PASTA TO IMPRESS

*Here is a repertoire of simple but stylish pasta dishes that make you look good, whether you're out to impress friends, family, your boss or your date!*

Spicy Garlic Prawns with Cherry Tomatoes
**(See page 73)**
Pan-Roast Chicken with Garlic & Shallots
**(See page 84)**
Seafood Extravaganza
**(See page 77)**
Scallops with Creme Fraiche & Dill
**(See page 72)**
Smoked Salmon with White Wine, Cream & Chives
**(See page 70)**
Wild Mushroom Persillade
**(See page 57)**

## PASTA FOR CROWDS

*Easy and economical, pasta can feed hoards of hungry mouths, without breaking the bank or causing sleepless nights. Refer to our Think Ahead notes.*

Spinach & Ricotta Lasagne
**(See page 118)**
Mushroom Al Forno
**(See page 60)**
Tomato & Mozzarella Al Forno
**(See page 39)**
Roast Vegetables Al Forno
**(See page 141)**
Classic Lasagne Al Forno
**(See page 95)**

## SUMMER WEEKEND PASTA

*Light dishes with bright tastes for lazy lunches in the sunshine.*

Fresh Tomato Sauce with Pesto
**(See page 37)**
Aubergine with Garlic, Basil & Pine Nuts
**(See page 137)**
Chilli Prawns
**(See page 70)**
Fresh Tomato, Red Onion & Basil
**(See page 33)**
Red Pesto with Rocket
**(See page 31)**
Spicy Garlic Scallops
**(See page 73)**

# THE SKILLS - TOP TIPS

**PEELING TOMATOES**
Cut a small cross on the base of each tomato. Drop tomatoes into boiling water. Remove when you see the edges of the cross begin to loosen, 10-20 seconds, depending on the ripeness. Drain, then immerse tomatoes in cold water. Peel off the loosened skins, using the tip of a knife.

**SOAKING DRIED MUSHROOMS**
Place mushrooms in a small bowl and add boiling water to cover. Leave for 30 minutes.

**SEEDING TOMATOES**
Cut the tomato in half crosswise. Gently squeeze each tomato half, pushing out the seeds with your fingertips.

**PEELING A GARLIC CLOVE**
Set the flat side of the knife on top and strike it with your fist. This action will loosen the skin, allowing it to peel away easily. Discard the skin.

## CHOPPING AN ONION

Peel the onion, leaving the root end on. Cut the onion in half and lay one half, cut side down, on a chopping board. With a sharp knife, cut horizontally towards the root end, and then vertically. Be sure to cut just to the root but not through it. Finally, cut the onion crosswise into diced pieces.

## PEELING PEPPERS

Grill peppers under a preheated grill. Turn as needed until blackened on all sides, 10-15 minutes. Place in a plastic bag or a bowl with a plate on top and allow to cool. Peel off the skin using the tip of a small knife. Cut the peppers into quarters and remove the core. Scrape away seeds and discard.

# THE CHOP - SIZE GUIDE
*All pictures shown are in proportion*

ROUGHLY CHOPPED PARSLEY

FINELY CHOPPED PARSLEY

DICED TOMATO

DICED CARROT AND CELERY

**SLICED ONION**

**CHOPPED ONION**

**FINELY CHOPPED ONION**

**FINELY CHOPPED GARLIC**

# NOTES FROM THE COOKS ON INGREDIENTS

**ANCHOVY FILLETS** can be soaked in milk for 10 minutes before using if you find the flavour too pungent. Use ½ tsp of anchovy paste as an alternative to 1 anchovy fillet when called for as an ingredient in a cooked pasta sauce.

**BUTTER** should always be unsalted when working with the recipes in this book.

**CAPERS** must be drained before using when they come packed in brine. We prefer to use capers preserved in salt, which are harder to find but worth the effort, since they retain more of their natural flavour than those packed in brine. Capers preserved in salt must be rinsed and dried on paper towels before using.

**CHEESES** that are most suitable for the pasta pantry are discussed in more detail on page 46. **Fontina** is a semi-soft cheese made from cow's milk with an aromatic flavour and great melting properties. Look for authentic Italian fontina when possible and avoid the more widely available Danish variety. Its name is a derivative of *fondere* – to melt.
**Gruyere** is a hard Swiss cheese with a sweet, nutty flavour. It melts without becoming oily or rubbery and is a good alternative to fontina cheese.
**Parmesan** is a hard Italian cheese with a rich, sharp flavour that is nothing like the stale, acrid taste of ready-grated parmesan sold in a tub. Always buy Italian Parmesan. Buy in a piece and grate it as required. See page 46 for further information.
**Pecorino Romano** is a hard Italian cheese with a tangy, piquant flavour that pairs well with the spicy pasta sauces originating from southern Italy. Use Parmesan as an alternative.
**Provolone** is a cheese made from cow's milk. It has a light ivory colour, a mild flavour and a smooth texture.

**Mascarpone** is the creamiest of Italian cheeses. It was originally made as a fresh cheese only in the winter months, and had to be consumed within a couple of days. Now it is manufactured with a UHT process and sold in tubs, allowing it to be a 'long-life' product. It does not have the same superior taste of the highly perishable 'fresh', but is an adequate substitute.
**Ricotta** is used extensively in Italian cooking. If you can, buy it fresh from authentic Italian delicatessens, but be sure to taste it for freshness before buying and to use it with in 48 hours.

**CRUSHED CHILLI FLAKES** are a widely available hot seasoning often used as an ingredient in pasta sauces. Referred to as peperoncino in Italian.

**DRIED BREADCRUMBS** should be made with good white bread that is 2 to 3 days old. Cut the bread into pieces and pulse in a food processor or a blender until reduced to fine crumbs. Spread crumbs on a baking tray and bake in a preheated 150°C (300°F) Gas 2 oven for a 2 to 3 minutes, until dry and crisp. Make a large batch and store in an airtight container for up to 1 month.

**EGGS** are always large eggs. Recipes made with uncooked egg, such as Carbonara (see page 88) and Cream and Parmesan (see page 49) should not be made for children or elderly persons.

**FLOUR** for making fresh pasta is ideally Italian pasta flour, **Tipo 00/Doppio Zero** (double zero), which can be found at some supermarkets and in Italian speciality stores. Alternatively, use plain flour. **Semolina** flour is a useful addition when making fresh pasta dough. Sprinkle liberally over freshly made pasta to prevent it from sticking. We recommend buying Italian semolina whenever possible.

GARLIC are always medium-sized cloves unless we indicate otherwise.

LEMONS for lemon zest should be organic whenever possible since they are unwaxed and unsprayed.

MUSHROOMS should never be rinsed in water. To clean mushrooms properly, simply wipe gently with a damp towel. See page 56 for more information on the varieties of mushrooms best suited for pasta.

NUTMEG is sold ground or whole. We recommend buying whole nutmeg and grating it freshly as needed. The flavour of freshly grated nutmeg is vastly superior to anything ground.

PINE NUTS are the most flavourful when they are toasted over medium heat in a dry cast-iron frying pan until golden and fragrant, 5 minutes. Shake the pan frequently. Remove from the pan immediately.

PRAWNS when large should be deveined after removing the shells. Run a small, sharp knife over the top edge of the peeled prawn and rinse away the grit.

PROSCIUTTO is an Italian air-dried, salt cured ham. See page 80 for more information.

OLIVES - see information about the olive varieties best suited for pasta on page 98.

SUN-DRIED TOMATOES are most commonly sold marinated in oil; drain before using. We like to use demi-sec tomatoes that are partly dried and not preserved in olive oil. These must be reconstituted in equal parts vinegar and water for 3 hours. Dry with paper towels and use immediately, or store covered in extra virgin olive oil with 2 or 3 cloves of garlic.

SEA SALT is always preferred in all recipes. Buy it in flakes or crystals. See page 21 for more information.

# INDEX

## MAIL ORDER SOURCES

**THE SHOP AT WEST COUNTRY
FINE FOODS**
East Farm, Codford St. Mary
Nr. Warminster, Wiltshire BA12 OPJ
T: (01985) 850524
www.westcountryfinefoods.co.uk
Email: the shop@wcff.co.uk
*Pasta flour, fresh wild mushrooms, pancetta,
Pecorino and other Italian cheese. Extensive
selection of gourmet foods available for mail order.*

**CARLUCCIO'S**
35 Rose Street, Covent Garden
London WC2E 9EB
T: 020 7580 3050
F: 020 7580 3070
www.carluccios.com
Email: theoffice@carluccios.com
*Specialist Italian ingredients, including pasta
flour, capers in salt and Castelluccio lentils.*

**DIVERTIMENTI**
227-229 Brompton Road
London SW3 2EP
T: 020 7581 8065
F: 020 7823 9429
www.divertimenti.co.uk
Email: brompton@divertimenti.co.uk

33-34 Marylebone High Street
London W1U 4PT
T: 020 7935 0689
F: 020 7224 0058
www.divertimenti.co.uk
Email: marylebone@divertimenti.co.uk
*Catalogue available. Kitchenware, tableware
and gourmet ingredients.*

**TAKE IT FROM HERE**
Unit 04
Beta Way
Thorpe Industrial Estate
Egham
Surrey TW20 8RZ
T: 0800 137 064
F: 01784 477 813
www.fastweb.co.uk/takeitfromhere/index.htm
Email: sales@takeitfromhere.co.uk
*Catalogue available. Olive oil, capers in
salt, pasta.*

*Index compiled by Sue Bosanko*

# HOW WE MAKE OUR BOOKS

In 1983, a tiny bookstore with a unique concept opened in London's Notting Hill. BOOKS FOR COOKS is a bookstore run by cooks for cooks, selling only cookbooks, teaching cooking classes, cooking from the books and serving up the results in a tiny restaurant among the bookshelves.

I work in the store, cook in the kitchen, and teach in the school. It's true that I acquired my technical training as a professional chef, but to my mind, my real culinary education began the day I crossed the threshold of Books For Cooks. It's from my students and customers that I learn most about the way people live, cook, and eat today, and it's this experience that informs the way we make our books. Real food for real life is our motto. Each title is specially devised to meet the needs of today's busy cooks.

I'm lucky enough to work in a team of dedicated food lovers. We research, test, photograph, write, design, and edit our books from start to finish. All the ingredients are bought from ordinary shops and tested in a domestic kitchen. Our recipes are designed to be cooked at home. Oh yes, and it's all real food in the photographs!

You can write, phone, fax or e-mail us any time. We'd love to hear from you.

*Enic*

**BOOKS FOR COOKS**
4 BLENHEIM CRESCENT
LONDON W11 1NN
TEL: 020 7221 1992
FAX: 020 7221 1517

**info@booksforcooks.com**